BRICK BY BRICK
ON THE ROAD THROUGH
OZ.

RECOVERY FROM SEXUAL ABUSE TRAUMA

Revised edition of a monograph originally written in 1993 for
The Union Institute and University

G. G. Bolich, Ph.D.

Psyche's

Press

Psyche's Press
Raleigh, NC
©1993, 2008 G. G. Bolich

ISBN 978-0-6151-6702-2

Table of Contents

Introduction
Magical Imaginings

Prelude to an Opera

Songs sing stories; some shout as they soar.
Others whisper along a dusky path,
Searching for a way home.

In Kansas, stormy weather bends
Life's journey through dust and haze,
And twists a young girl's way.

But every cyclone ends.
The circling, winding ways
Spiral to a rainbow's arching touch.

A Kansas twister is a door
To a magical pot of gold made
In Oz.

Storm Warning

Be warned: this is not an easy book.

This book is about the trauma—and the healing—of sexual abuse. I have made no attempt to trick anyone onto a path with promises of instant success or sure-fire answers. Much of the material is challenging to digest and will require time, reflection, and earnest effort. Most worthwhile things do.

This book will be useful for both therapists and survivors. I hope survivors will team with their therapists to explore this imaginative journey together. Rest assured: this *is* the story of a journey, an odyssey through storms and turmoil, through familiar and unknown spaces, to reach a place where all is well. Along the way we will encounter many other travelers, some of who will pose obstacles and others who will gift us with opportunities for friendship and love. This is the story of Dorothy of Kansas and her companions in Oz. But it is my story, too—and perhaps it will be yours.

In the few pages of this introduction I want to explain why I chose Dorothy's story. I want you to understand what her story can do for you. To accomplish that is going to mean speaking a bit about language and experience, about the transforming power of metaphor and story. Although this material is not necessary for you to benefit from the journey the rest of the book will take you on, it will lend you a clearer grasp of why that journey works. So, if you will, sit with me a few minutes before we start walking the yellow brick road.

Imagine

Once upon a time there was a little girl from Kansas named Dorothy.

When I was a child this story captured my imagination, just as it has done for millions of children since L. Frank Baum first penned it in the early years of the twentieth century. Later, the story became even better known through perennial appearances on television of the 1939 movie based on Baum's novel. Today there is scarcely anyone in our culture who is not familiar with *The Wizard of Oz*. Still, in my own mind, this has become *my* story, because it speaks to me in an especially personal way. Without trying to allegorize its every detail, the story of Dorothy has suggested to me some key ideas I have found useful in my own life and in the lives of those I work with, fellow survivors of sexual abuse trauma.

When Dorothy visits Oz she is not alone. I am there beside her, and I go back often to repeat with her that magical journey along the yellow brick road. Dorothy's story draws me into her experience in such a way as to experience it myself as though it were my own. But even more importantly, in experiencing her story I write my own, and as often as I visit her story I act to rewrite my own. Dorothy's journey has become a vehicle for change in my own life's adventure.

Stories change us as they become our own. We are all built in such a manner that we respond to experience. But we may not always be conscious of how profound an effect is accomplished upon us by experiences of our imagination. In at least some respects, the body treats imaginative experiences as though they actually happen in the world. When, for example, we imagine a sexual encounter our body may respond as though the flesh and blood stimulus was present. We become aroused. When we view a movie's tender scene of lovers parting, our own feelings are stirred and changes in our body chemistry take place as though the actual experience was happening to us. We become sad. Our identification with others' experiences involves us in experiencing something very like what they are experiencing. This power is invoked through story and metaphor.

Metaphor

Now indulge me a moment while I wax a little philosophical. I want to explain what metaphors are all about and why they matter. If you are a survivor of sexual abuse, you may want to skip this section, or even to press on to chapter 1, where our journey with Dorothy properly begins. I won't object. (Therapists, *you* are not excused!) But if you linger here with me a little while, I think a deeper understanding of what this book is all about is possible.

All of us find certain stories draw us in so that we become a part of them. What has happened is that we have participated in a metaphorical experience. As survivors of sexual abuse, our own stories often seem muddled or even lost. Paradoxically, we may be a people especially drawn to the stories of others. Perhaps in their stories we seek our own. Such wonderful power needs to be comprehended if we are to derive full benefit from it.

What are metaphors? They are imaginative comparisons in which something is treated as though it were something else. The purpose may be to show how two things are alike or how they are different. But the key element is that 'A' is treated *as if* it were 'B.' We use metaphors in everyday language. They help us understand unseen qualities. So, for example, when we say something like, 'Our God is a mighty rock,' we don't mean literally that we worship a large stone. We mean that God has some of the qualities we associate with a stone, such as strength we can shelter in. God is *not* a rock, but the comparison between God and a rock is truthful in what it shows us.

Metaphors are an important way of speaking both because they permit us new insights and because they are so natural to us. Indeed, various philosophers and scientists tell us that the human mind is built for making and using metaphors. They are pervasive in our thinking and language, shaping how we conceive the world's relations and structure, and making rich how we talk about these things. When metaphors are brought together, like separate notes set in a melody, they establish the songs we call stories. Through stories human beings are able to tell complex truths in memorable, easily told fashion. Such stories do everything from helping us understand and explain ourselves to comprehending and describing the universe. In so doing, stories teach, challenge, question, entertain, and uplift us. In short, metaphors—and the stories they inhabit—are full-bodied, natural vehicles for carrying truths that appeal to both mind and soul.

Yet metaphor and story do more. They actually change us. Metaphors are able to transform us precisely because they *embody* experience. When we use metaphors, we relate things in ways that alter our perceptions and deepen our experience of them. When we tell stories, we wrap ourselves in another's flesh. To the degree we succeed in yielding ourselves to another body's experiencing we find changes taking place in our own body. Metaphorical experience is powerful and dangerous. We all do it, and done properly it can help us greatly.

Therapists rely on metaphorical—*as if*—experiences to help their clients. As a survivor of trauma I realize that no one else can ever know exactly what I have been through. I'm right of course, but correct in a way that can make me feel isolated and weak. But certain experiences of therapy have shown me this perception is not the whole truth. Though my experience is uniquely mine, others have shared it. They have listened to my story and used their imagination to enter into it. This peculiarly helpful use of imagination is called *empathy*. Through empathy someone is able to stand alongside another in that person's experience, but without being swept away by it. An empathic person like a good therapist becomes an anchor and a safe harbor—a partner and support as I undergo the turbulent storm of my own feelings and memories.

As a result my own experience is changed. I no longer feel isolated and weak. The presence of empathic others—folk willing to be changed by my story as they lend me their strength—comforts me. In turn, I learn how to be empathic toward others. Indeed, as one survivor among others, I have often experienced connecting to someone else's story more strongly than I sometimes do to my own. I am able to engage feelings for them I often cannot muster for myself. I have entered their experience metaphorically, and we both are changed.

I draw upon such experiences as a therapist. I know that even though I have not had my client's experience, I can imaginatively enter her experience. Through *as if*, metaphorical experience I can stand alongside her. Such empathy is the most essential factor in successful therapy. It utilizes the full power of metaphorical experience, a power able to change every party involved, but one that has certain intrinsic safeguards. Think of it: I can stand alongside someone else in her experience without being overwhelmed by it. I can do this because my experience has the safety of being metaphorical. Now this may sound incredible. How can experiencing something as scary as sexual abuse be safe even if done only imaginatively? My clients commonly fear to share their stories with me because they do not wish to see me hurt as they have been hurt. Yet I know I am only pretending to have this experience—and that protects me. But this is not a silly game. My entering into their stories fills me with feeling even as my knowledge that the story is not my own creates just enough psychological space to keep firm footing. The sum of all this is that the *as if* experience grants me access to things helpful to my client.

To some degree, we all are acquainted with the kinds of imaginative experience I am talking about. Some of us, though, are better at it than others. This is why two people sitting together watching the same movie may have very different reactions. One has joined the experience on the screen and is being changed by it while the other remains a passive, unmoved observer. Little happens in the body of the passive observer except those changes associated with the posture and inactivity of merely watching.

But look what transpires in the other! The blood pressure may rise and dive, perspiration flow freely, blood flush the face, and the heart beat wildly. Awareness of peripheral factors—like the bored companion sitting in the next seat—fades as involvement in what is happening on the screen becomes a matter of more intense personal identification. Metaphorical experience is not just in the mind—it happens in the body, too. That is another reason it works so well for those of us wounded in our bodies by trauma. Metaphor can help heal both mind and body.

We can all learn how to better use metaphorical experience. This book is practical training in the art. It will help those of us who are survivors to better connect with our own experience through using Dorothy's story as a vehicle. It will aid those of us who are therapists, or friends or family of survivors, to meet survivors on common, neutral ground to face experiences that seem too hard to face. For all of us, Oz is an enchanted place where we can learn more about Kansas and eventually find our way home.

Yet there are warnings we must heed. The raw power of metaphor, especially embedded in a larger story, means it behooves us to choose the ones we participate in very carefully. Metaphors can separate us from ordinary experience and become the sacred space where we experience salvation. Such power demands proper respect. Entering Dorothy's story is not without risk.

Yet their power is not the only reason we need to be careful. Metaphors are messy. Saying that 'God is a mighty rock' may be a nice image but it lacks scientific precision. Dorothy's way along the yellow brick road is not straightforward and eludes scientific measurement. The openness of metaphors, their pronounced tendency to cluster together to tell stories, makes them tempting. Those same qualities make them frustrating to those who want everything lined up neat and straight. That includes all of us who want order to overcome our chaos.

But the universe is what it is. Our experience is messy. The truths we learn in life don't always fit along neat lines. The deepest lessons seem round about and convoluted. So we resonate more with stories than summaries of facts. Metaphors speak truths facts cannot utter.

Fortunately, there is a philosophy of science built upon the use of metaphorical experience as the doorway into truths that measurements never fully capture. Back slightly before MGM turned Dorothy's story into movie magic, a fellow named Hans Vaihinger articulated a philosophy sometimes called 'fictionalism,' but better known as 'as if' thinking. The former label is not derogatory. Vaihinger knew that something need not be factually correct in order to have practical importance. In other words, something need not be rooted in the domain of height, length, and depth in order to be powerfully useful in human experience. The best truths *work*; they change us in healthy ways.

To treat what we know is factually false *as if* it were true may lead to better knowing the truths that matter most. Even science, Vaihinger pointed out, uses fiction. In fact, science can be seen as a kind of storytelling. Mental health professionals scientifically apply the art of storytelling to help clients navigate their experiences in healthier ways. This would not work if the stories were untrue. Metaphorical truth depends on confirmation in immediate experience. Help is where we find it, and for those of us who have survived the trauma of sexual abuse, the journey through Oz justifies itself in an experience that brings understanding and healing.

This volume relies on *as if* thinking. To travel with Dorothy requires imagination. We are going to do more than brave the power of metaphor, we are going to count on it, enlisting it in the service of understanding what we have endured and where we can go from here. The messiness of metaphor only mirrors the universe of human experience. *Life* is messy.

But here is the decisive advantage metaphor and story gives us. If we choose wisely, metaphors and stories can grant us *safe passage* through the dangers we encounter. Our own stories must be faced. But, rooted in all too real experience, their power shakes us to the core. Dorothy's story offers us a way to safely connect with our own. As we make her story ours, ours becomes hers. Through the magic of *as if* thinking, two journeys mingle along the same road. This grants us greater safety to face our own Kansas trauma, find friends and allies in Oz, and walk the yellow brick road to our own recovery.

Dorothy & I

But why choose *Dorothy's* story? Let me offer three reasons among many I might mention. First, Dorothy's story has the safety of well-worn familiarity. We know how it turns out. Despite every difficulty, Dorothy triumphs! Second, her story—like all enduring ones—is organized around clear and compelling truths. We are drawn to the truth that real power resides in us, that home is always close to the heart, and that unlikely allies can surface around us at anytime and in any guise. The truths of Dorothy's story are ones we all need. Finally, Dorothy's experiences are tremendously suggestive of experiences common to survivors of all kinds of trauma, including sexual abuse. Her story is filled with metaphors that will shed light and comfort as I explain sexual abuse trauma and the road of recovery.

Trauma of any kind is a major plot point in any life story. Sexual trauma complicates the story being written by not merely adding a twist to the plot, but by altering the principal characters. From that point forward everything is different. The rest of the story becomes one both of recovery and progress, a move to restore and a push to move on. In accompanying Dorothy from Kansas to Oz and back again, we may find our own movements mirrored. Our Kansas and our Oz benefit from her experience.

For me, Dorothy's story has been an especially magical one. But I would not wish anyone to conclude it is the only story that has helped me, nor that every story proves useful to me. Nor do I want anyone to think that it is only by analyzing images, such as the tornado or the yellow brick road, that I find help. Dorothy's story is a full-bodied experience in which I participate as though the events were my own. Certain images stay with me, of course, and in them I have invested special significance. They have thus become even more my own because I have seen and felt them in ways other than Dorothy does. As mine, I have the freedom to do with them whatever they permit me to do. You will find the same is true for you.

Dorothy's experience speaks to us whenever we experience it as our own. This is not a psychotic act; it remains an imaginative act because we remain aware that the two experiences are not the same. We are doing what therapists and fellow survivors do all the time—finding the truth in another's story. We act *as if* Dorothy's experience is ours in order to change our own experience. Participating in metaphor becomes a purposeful act. It remains our decision how and to what degree we choose to enter. At the same time, having entered we become subject to the life of the metaphor and it may take us unexpected directions. Serendipity—unexpected delight—has her home in metaphor.

Acting as though Dorothy's story were ours, while ours is still in place, brings about new insights, an altered perception, and a series of changes that moves our own stories along, for better or worse. The advantage to us is that we don't have to go through a Kansas twister and slay wicked witches in order to profit from what Dorothy learns. The tapestry of Dorothy's story allows us to walk the yellow brick road, face its many challenges, and emerge safe and strong for our own travels. Her story sets a special, magical mirror in which we see our own stories differently. In this way the metaphorical act is not only true, it is the kind of truth that sets one free.

Chapter 1

DOROTHY

Confession

I thought it was only little boys
who were made of snails and puppy dog tails.
But there skips Dorothy of Oz
in her daisy frock and flouncing pigtails.

Who thought girls, too, were made of sterner stuff?

Dorothy

One day Dorothy of Kansas found herself caught in a tornado. Now a similar event happens more frequently than we might wish to imagine. If we believe the numbers tossed about by most sources, some one-in-three girls by age 18 are caught in the gritty groping of a storm called sexual abuse. Nor are girls alone. While the figures swirl more confusingly concerning boys, some people who work frequently with survivors of sexual abuse believe the number of boys caught up in this storm is nearly as great. Any way it is looked at, the tornado sweeping the land is a dark, dark wind.

What happened to Dorothy? She found herself in a strange new land. Her old ways of looking at the world had to change because this land of Oz into which she had fallen was not at all like the Kansas she called home. Tornados have a way of changing landscapes. Those who have been swept up into the sexual abuse funnel know that quite well. The world changes.

It matters not a whit to me that the story of Dorothy told by L. Frank Baum was not written about sexual abuse. Stories tend to take on their own life and spawn meanings never imagined by the first storyteller. What matters very much to me is that in this story of a girl named Dorothy I find meanings that speak to the experience of something defining in my own life and in the lives of many I have known. Dorothy experienced elements of change helpful to my own journey. Whatever Dorothy's tornado was, mine was sexual abuse. She found herself in Oz, and that is as good a name as any for a land that most definitely is not Kansas anymore.

But did Dorothy really go to Oz? The storyteller who brought to life the story of Dorothy, wrote that she actually traveled to another land. The movie, which made the story famous around the world, pictures the whole experience of Oz as a dream. Perhaps Dorothy imagined a place of safety, a realm where magic and magical friends could give her the power to accomplish what she thought she could not manage upon the wind swept plains of Kansas. In technical terms, a therapist might say that Dorothy 'dissociated.' Her experience of the tornado was so overwhelming that her mind could only preserve itself by breaking that experience into smaller, separate, manageable bits. Some parts may have stayed in Kansas; others went to Oz. There is magic in dissociation, because at least some troubling sensations, perceptions or memories flee the real world of painful experience and take up temporary residence in some safer place. For some girls and boys this might mean a kind of leaving from the body to reside, for instance, in a bare light bulb on the ceiling above while riding out the storm. It does not really matter where we go so long as it is safer than where we have been.

Oz

We need not concern ourselves whether Dorothy imagined Oz or not, because it is her experience of Oz that has much to teach us. Oz is not Kansas. In Oz there are forests of trees that talk to little girls, fields of poppies that stretch as far as the eye can see, and a great Emerald City. Connecting all is a simple yellow brick road. When I journey with Dorothy to Oz the yellow brick road becomes what I walk on too. Perhaps I invest somewhat different meanings than Dorothy does in this road. Perhaps I use it as a symbol in a way that never occurs to her. But this is my road as much as hers. I may have begun by walking in her footsteps, but somewhere along the way the steps became my own and it is my feet that tell me what the bricks are all about.

Throughout this book the yellow brick road wends its way through Dorothy's adventure and my own. Along the way it brushes alongside a great many things, including not a few ideas that may have nothing at all to do with Dorothy but dot the landscape of my own experience of Oz. If I appear to move freely in and out of Oz the appearance is not deceiving. I am not forgetting that Oz is not Kansas, that I am not Dorothy, and that even the best metaphors are not meant to substitute for life in this mundane world. *Metaphors and stories invite us in not in order to escape our world but to transform and enhance it.*

The Big Lesson of Oz—and of Life

Every story has a central movement, a thrust that keeps it headed toward some form of resolution. Dorothy's story is no different. As near the story's end she whispers again and again, "There's no place like home . . . there's no place like home," she underscores in a wistful, but no less emphatic manner what her journey has been about. From the moment of her arrival, Dorothy seeks not Oz, but Kansas. This is a remarkable testimony to Dorothy's strength and rootedness in reality. She never forgets that she is just a visitor in Oz; her real home remains in Kansas. No tornado can keep her from reclaiming her own proper place.

Dorothy is never deceived. From the moment her whirling house thumps down hard in Oz, Dorothy knows a change has taken place. "I have a feeling we're not in Kansas anymore," she tells Toto. Of course, her arrival is hardly inconspicuous. Her landing brings about the death of one wicked witch and sets another against her. Oz might be different from Kansas, but it is no less dangerous. Fortunately, a good witch, Glinda, sets the dead witch's ruby slippers on Dorothy's feet and points her to the yellow brick road, which leads to the Emerald City and the fabled wizard there.

Dorothy & the Wizard

Dorothy has high hopes for the wizard. After all, she is herself just a little girl in a far, far away place. He is the mighty wizard, ruler of a magical land, reputed to be as wise as he is powerful. As she sets her steps upon the yellow brick road she pins her hopes on his delivering her. The irony is that through her journey and the adventures it brings her she comes to realize for her companions that the qualities they seek in external things are within them all along. Scarecrow's diploma only superficially represents the brains he has shown at every moment. Tin Woodsman's watch may provide a tick-tock to delight the ear, but his heart has already been heard in his compassion along the way to the Emerald City. Lion's courage does not reside in the medal the wizard presents him, but in the majestic actions by which he risks himself to help others. Yet seeing that what her friends covet resides in them all along, Dorothy remains blind a little longer to the same truth about herself.

She knows where she wants to be—Kansas—but is uncertain how to get there. She believes the great wizard possesses the means to deliver her. So in setting out along the yellow brick road, Dorothy embarks upon a salvation quest, one that will soon involve yet other quests and lead to many adventures. Like any tornado survivor, Dorothy's journey proves winding and filled with challenging obstacles. Like any traveler, she finds those who mean to help her— Scarecrow, Tin Woodsman, and Lion—and others who mean her harm— notably the wicked witch. Like any person who keeps on walking, Dorothy sees many strange, perplexing things. But most of all, like anyone who refuses to give up, Dorothy reaches her destination, fulfills all of her quests, and learns the one great lesson offered by Oz and life alike.

Dorothy eventually discovers that *the ability to be where one wants to be is within each of us all along.* Now to be sure the story talks about her ruby slippers. But is that where the power really lies? Does clicking shoes together three times do any more than unbind the power in Dorothy that resides there from the start? The nature of magic is making external what is present invisibly, internally, moment by moment. That is why wielders of magic speak of spells of making and spells of unbinding. The former, using things like naming, bring together loosely related elements within an object or person so as to form a unity—a whole greater than the sum of the parts. Thus a making spell is one of power. But so, too, is an unbinding spell. Such a spell looses what is restricted so that its essence, in all its natural power, stands revealed.

The magic of Dorothy's slippers is unbinding magic. Through participating in metaphors—such as experiencing Dorothy's story as if my own—I have found much magic of both the making and unbinding variety. The two kinds of magic, I have learned, are of the same nature in respect to what they aim to do. Both enhance what is already present in such a way that the result seems brand new. It is a birthing and rebirthing—what religious folk call regeneration. It is the act and the moment of salvation when the resources within are collected together, or released, and the world inside and outside us is never the same again.

But salvation for most of us comes when we stop looking for rescue from outside ourselves and we begin to attend to what lies within us.

The Yellow Brick Road

What lies within each of us is the power to talk and to walk. We are the author of our own story, the pilot of our own course. I am not so naïve as to suggest that life does not present us with many significant challenges not of our making, nor the child of our desires. But what we do with each challenge belongs entirely to us. If it is true that our feet are often set on paths not of our own choosing, it is equally true that we have the power to change the nature of the road we are walking. If we must, we can build our own road, brick by brick.

We *can* and *must* rescue ourselves, step by step.

We can build our road day by day, and at the close of each day we still have the materials to build a warm brick home to shield us against the cold, dark night. Each of us has within all we require to be our own safe place. No matter what our experience of home, we can make for ourselves our own home within, a place of nurture, warmth, and emotional satisfaction. We may have to build the hearth and light the fire ourselves, but we will be just as warm as anyone else.

The yellow brick road that Dorothy walks in Oz is both path and home along the way. It not only guides her steps, it provides all she needs. Along its length she finds companions. The fields and forests that border it provide food and shelter. Though Dorothy does not have to lay the bricks (as we may have to do), she still has to walk them. And she decides when and where to walk and rest. She makes the road her own.

For Dorothy in Oz going home first means having to find and walk the yellow brick road. It is only at the end of it that she finds herself in her fullness. Those of us who experience sexual abuse often long for a clearly marked road to follow. Believing it leads to a wonderful wizard brightens our steps. But all too often our reality is much harder. It involves not merely walking a road but building it brick by brick. Laying bricks is tough, thankless work. Yet if it is a road to get where we want to be that needs building, then waiting around for someone else to build it seems rather chancy. Undoubtedly, some of us are better road builders than others, but it is getting where we want to be that matters, not how pretty the road is, nor even how straight.

Even Dorothy's ready-made road proves a winding one. Perhaps every worthwhile road has to have its curves and bumps to remind us to watch where we are going. Mine is constantly surprising me, and I can never see what is beyond the bend ahead. Perhaps yours is like that too. I sometimes weary of the journey and I often tire of having to build a path leading places I still only dream about. But when I put one foot ahead of the other and take another step forward I have an immense satisfaction in the process of what I am accomplishing.

I must admit, though, as a bricklayer I make a wonderful poet. Yet though my mind wanders and I find myself readier to dream of pillowed clouds and candy dragons than to get my hands dirty, I somehow manage amidst my sighs to lay a brick here and there. And every brick brings me one step closer to where I want to be. I measure my days by the bricks I lay, not by the number I wish I had placed. While keeping my eyes on the destination ahead, I don't forget to occasionally look back and praise myself for how far I have come.

Brick by brick we can build our own roads. We do not have to rely on anyone to do the work for us. Indeed, making ourselves dependent on others for rescue is risky business at best. I like the satisfaction of seeing what my own labor builds. I like feeling strong and capable. So what if my brick road is not as shiny as someone else's. It is taking me where I want to go and *it is all mine*.

Remember Dorothy on the yellow brick road. Sometimes she skips along with a glow on her face answering the sunny smile in the sky. Other times she is bent over in fear, anxiously searching for breaks among the storm clouds. At all times, though, she steps so as to keep her feet on the path. If nothing else, having to build our own road brick by brick makes it that much easier to stay close to the path.

Chapter 2

OF BRICKS AND ROADS

If Dorothy was Me

Auntie Em, you shoulda knowed better,
when that witch came for Toto.
When you gave him away in silence,
you silenced my voice, too.

Did you want me to run away?

Uncle Henry, you shoulda knowed better,
with the twister barreling down.
You shoulda waited a few moments longer,
just a few. . . only a few .

Oh, how could you risk me that way?

Why, oh why didn't I know any better?
How, oh how could I be such a fool?
It isn't witches or twisters,
but myself who's to blame.

I shoulda been better that awful day.

What Are Bricks For?

Had one of us been Dorothy, I wonder how we might have responded to the invitation to walk the yellow brick road. Consider what an upsetting time the last little while has been. Toto is snatched away, Dorothy recovers him, then runs away herself. Persuaded to return home she is caught in a Kansas twister, endures a frightening ride, lands with a thud, kills a witch in the process, and is stunned to discover a wondrous place where she is first greeted with singing praise, then threatened with destruction by another witch. Finally, a third witch shows up and bids her walk a strange road that starts with a tiny circle and spirals out into a strange land. I fear I would have been a bit overwhelmed by it all.

Frankly, I can see myself collapsing to the ground and having a good cry. After that, I can imagine mulling everything over and being both scared and mad. How did I get myself into this mess? Is this really *my* fault? Who's to blame?? I can picture my fingers clenching a loose brick, lifting it, and looking around for someone to throw it at.

Unfortunately, as immediately satisfying as that might sound, it won't get me one step closer to where I want to be. The bricks of the yellow brick road are better walked than thrown. Back here in Kansas, facing the reality of having survived a cyclone of another kind, I face the same temptation I might in Oz— and the same basic truth: I can throw bricks or use them for walking. All of us who have survived sexual abuse know the feelings of suddenly finding ourselves in a strange land and having to decide what to do next. Unfortunately, we often lack a clearly marked road such as Dorothy has. Instead, we have a pile of bricks, the disordered chaos of our experience and the choices we now face. We can start slinging them or building a road.

Sitting on the ground while we sling bricks is indulging in *blame*. The act of blaming can feel good. Blaming offers a kind of emotional release, and may even feel empowering when directed at others. But blame is an attack that avoids more responsible action. Blame succeeds chiefly at emoting, not moving. It is hard to attain the productive solution of walking the yellow brick road when we keep tearing up its bricks to use as weapons. Yet that is all blame does—it throws bricks rather than builds with them. The result is not merely destructive to others. It hurts us. I repeat: throwing bricks doesn't get us any further along the road ourselves. Only by first using the bricks for road building, then actually setting out along the way can we get where we want to be.

Walking to Get There Rather than Sitting in Blame

One of the marvelous things about walking is that no one can do it for us. It is not like being carried, where the breathing is never labored and our eyes can indulge themselves in looking at whatever they choose as long as they like. When walking, breathing often turns to panting and the eyes have to pay attention to the path. But if walking can be strenuous it also can be rewarding. What a sense of accomplishment to reach the end of the trail and look back at where one has been! I rather imagine Dorothy, back in Kansas, finds occasion to thrill with pride over her long journey.

Dorothy is a walker, not a sitter. It shows right from the start of her time in Oz. One thing I admire about her is that she never wastes time on figuring out who to blame for her situation. There is no sitting around trying to figure out who she can throw bricks at. Instead, she squares her shoulders, gathers up Toto, and sets off with a bounce of determination. One way or another she seems to grasp very quickly that it does not matter who is to blame for her being in Oz, because it is up to her to do what she can to get to where she wants to be. Dorothy concerns herself with *her* responsibility and lets others manage their own. That makes sense to me. After all, anxiety often results either from our taking on what does not belong to us at all, or taking on more than is proper even when the root of it is properly our responsibility.

So Dorothy spares herself a waste of precious time and energy by avoiding the tempting distraction of blaming and getting on with the walking. In a land populated by a wicked witch determined to do her harm this seems to me a very wise decision. If we are going to walk our paths—even building our own yellow brick roads as we go—then we need to avoid useless distractions. Perhaps, then, we need to think this matter of blame through rather carefully.

Commonly, when we are abused the first to be blamed is our own self. Maybe years later, when 'recovery' begins, we may decide to blame others. Either way can lead to powerful experiences, On the other hand, both lead to *negative* experiences since blame does not lay bricks but merely throws them.

Can you imagine Dorothy in full blame mode? "It's all that wicked woman's fault! If she hadn't been so mean, taking Toto away, I wouldn't have been caught in the tornado." Or what about dear old Auntie Em, who stayed silent while Toto was bundled away and Dorothy's trust was compromised? Or Uncle Henry, who gave up the search for Dorothy and locked the root cellar's doors against the tornado with Dorothy still outside? Those to whom she looked for protection let her down. If Dorothy wished to lay blame, she had plenty of plausible targets. Any number of times Dorothy had opportunity to put her troubles on someone else. When the marvelous wizard turned out to be a rather harmless fraud her disappointment might easily have led to a blaming anger: "Look at what you've put me through you wicked old man! My life will never be the same—I'm ruined because of you." But where would any of this blaming have left her?

Suppose Dorothy blamed herself. On viewing the dead witch in Oz she might have said, "Well, isn't that just like me, making a mess wherever I go? I can't do anything right! And now here I've murdered this witch and I'm sure to catch all kind of trouble for it." Or when she and her loyal companions were trapped in the castle of the wicked witch of the West she might have cried out, "What a terrible person I am! It isn't bad enough I can't keep myself out of trouble—now I've gone and brought disaster to my friends as well!" Surely her self-esteem would have plummeted. What does that mean in practical terms? Probably it would have meant feeling guilty and depressed. Instead of taking to the yellow brick road she might have collapsed in a heap beside it and brooded. If so, she might still be in Oz—at least until the witch of the West did her in!

Would Dorothy have been better off blaming the woman who took Toto, her beloved little dog? Surely many reasons could be advanced to justify placing the blame for her predicament on this woman. But what difference to Dorothy's situation would that have made? I will grant that such an act is a step ahead of blaming herself. Had she blamed Elvira Gulch, she might have temporarily elevated her mood knowing she was not at fault. But the bottom line would remain the same: she is stuck in Oz until she does something to get where she wants to be.

As for blaming the Wizard of Oz, I can only say *I* would certainly have things to say to him! In fact, so does Dorothy. She asserts her feelings about him and the fiasco, and she is right to do so. But that isn't blaming. Blaming is an attack upon someone rather than an expression of one's own internal state. The difference is important and not a mere quibbling over words. In blaming only destruction takes place. Blame cuts off and separates. Dorothy instead asserts her hurt, which starts the healing, while squarely acknowledging the reality of what has happened.

Blame in Sexual Abuse

I fear the distinction may still be elusive. Let's get very concrete and talk directly about sexual abuse. Every character in an abusive situation has a title. The one who abuses another is called 'abuser,' or 'perpetrator.' Those who assist the abuser actively, or who fail to act when they might have done so, are often called 'enablers.' The one who is abused is called 'the victim.' If this person makes an effort to constructively deal with the situation and somehow escapes it, then it is common to refer to her or him as a 'survivor' rather than as a victim. Trust me, it is far better being a survivor than a victim. Some call those who have succeeded in largely overcoming the negative effects of the experience, and who have managed to integrate the experience into their total life experience in a healing fashion, by the name 'prevailer.' Many of these roles can become the object of blame.

In blaming, what happens might look something like this. The abuser blames the victim for what is happening: "You seduced me." Or, perhaps: "You should enjoy this." (Meaning that if the victim does not like it, then she or he is to blame for being somehow defective.) There are numerous possibilities as to how victim blaming can happen. I doubt anyone disputes that this blaming is both inappropriate and harmful. It makes as much sense as blaming a victim in a random shooting for standing in the way of a bullet.

But certainly the victim has the right to blame the abuser. You will get no argument from me on that score. I agree. Victims have every right to blame the one who abused them for the abuse. I will even add, as I suggested above, that this is much better than blaming one's own self. But I don't need to vigorously exercise my every right in order to acknowledge I have it. I don't go out and burn the flag once a week because I have a right to do so. Do I jeopardize my right to burn the flag by not doing so? Of course not! I refrain from exercising this right because it is unproductive to uphold it, at least in all but unusual circumstances. I think the same is true of blaming. Outside of some exceptional situation, such as where blaming might be a key to experiencing a sense of liberation from the abuser's power, I find it counterproductive.

Angry?

That may seem a bitter pill to swish around in one's mouth. I am intimately familiar with the dance of anger that often surrounds thinking or feeling about the abuser. I am *not* suggesting the person who has been abused has no right to be angry or should not feel angry. We feel what we feel. But what we *do* with what we feel makes a difference. *Experience* the anger fully, and if there is an appropriate need to *express* the anger as well, then by all means do so. But use your anger constructively. Target any expression of anger where it will do you the most good rather than doing someone else a measure of harm. Think this way: to get where you want to go it is better to spent energy building than destroying. Liberate your energy so that your own yellow brick road can be both built and walked.

However, while we are paused to reflect on anger, let's be completely honest about this business of expressing it. While it is popular to encourage people to 'let it all hang out' when it comes to anger, this ventilation process is not all gains and no losses. In fact, psychological research reports that most of the time expressing anger makes people angrier, facilitates an angry attitude, and builds a habit of hostility. Are these outcomes we really want—or need? In the moment anger may feel liberating, flooding us with unexpected strength. But if it ends up making us worse off, feeling ultimately out of control, defeated and depressed, then what a price we've paid!

Once again, Dorothy is a good teacher. She gets mad on occasion, but she acts responsibly. When, for example, she meets the Cowardly Lion, she is at first afraid, for he presents himself as a bully. But when he chases after Toto, her anger overcomes her fear and she acts boldly to confront the danger she perceives. The result is that her action initiates a sequence of events leading to Lion confessing his cowardice, Dorothy engaging him in empathetic conversation (Dorothy a therapist?!), and his joining the band of companions. Again, in the Emerald City for the first audience with the wizard, Dorothy utilizes her anger to help her overcome her fear and to work constructively through the problem of the wizard's overbearing manner. In short, her anger helps her get unstuck, and that seems to me a most proper role for it.

Blame versus Assertion

When we blame someone else we attack them. We pour responsibility upon them like the proverbial coals of fire. If we are extremely lucky, they might even accept the blame and shrivel up beneath the heat. But what has been solved? Let's be painfully honest here. Even acknowledging responsibility for abusing us—an unlikely event at best—has limited usefulness for our healing. It validates us, but we still have to walk the path to being where and what we want to be. I don't diminish the value of an abuser's confession, but it should not be overvalued. Our abusers cannot give us either the journey we must make on our own or the destination we seek.

Blaming that is self-directed is even worse. Blame is actually other-directed even when aimed at the self. To blame myself means reducing myself to a target. It requires treating myself as an object. Demeaning myself hardly helps me even when the responsibility for a problem really does belong on my shoulders. But blaming myself for abuse by others is to grab what doesn't belong to me and to treat a lie as though it were true. This is self-reducing at the very time we most need self-building. We need to put our bricks down and start building our road.

Assertion is a better alternative. It is self-directed even when aimed at another. When we assert ourselves we are letting out into the external world some important thoughts and feelings birthed in our internal world. These children of our heart and mind go forth to represent us. They carry our hopes, our fears, our wishes, and our decisions. Instead of isolating us from others by distancing attacks, assertions invite the intimacy of response. They offer healing rather than destruction.

Now I grant that my wish as a victim or survivor may not be to bring healing between myself and my abuser. I may wish to heap coals upon the head, to see utter destruction and complete vengeance. I have that right. I'm just not enthusiastic about what exercising that right seems to indicate about me, or my prospects for the future. In assertion I can be honest about what happened. I can say, 'That hurt. I have paid a hell of a price for what happened. You had no right to do that to me." I can even choose to cut myself off from the abuser: "At least for now, and maybe forever, I don't want to have any part of my life touched by yours." In short, anything I might gain from blaming I can gain from asserting myself. At the same time I spare myself having to fix fault and being stuck right there.

Blaming leaves us stuck and that is no way to either build or walk our yellow brick road.

Response -Ability

So where does that leave responsibility? Let's go back to Dorothy. Rather than *place* responsibility, she *takes* responsibility. Moreover, in so doing, she accurately connects her responsibility to pursuing useful courses of action. Instead of placing responsibility for her situation on herself or others, which is a rather unproductive exercise when the goal is getting home, she takes responsibility for her actions to get her where she wants to be. I hope the connections are plain. Dorothy does *not* take responsibility for being in a bad spot and then place responsibility on others to rescue her. How would that help her? Obviously, Dorothy is a very wise young lady.

Putting responsibility on others is generally futile since we at best have limited control over their actions. Taking responsibility for others is even more futile, since our own life is big enough and hard enough to manage without the complication of trying to live someone else's life as well. Of course, it is frustrating to see where others who have responsibilities that affect us are acting irresponsibly. It may even be damaging to us, as it is with sexual abuse. We obviously are acting in our own best interests to assert our thoughts and feelings about how we are being affected. But if we become obsessed with someone else's responsibility, over which we have little if any influence, we are apt to become stuck and to find our own productive responsibility is left unfulfilled.

Yet many people find it difficult to see how anyone can talk about responsibility without also assigning blame. The logic seems to go like this: "If I am in a bad situation, someone must be responsible for my being there and they are the ones who properly should get me out of it. If naming names means blaming, then so be it. At least it's being honest." I find it hard to disagree. The logic seems impeccable to me. At the same time, a little voice keeps chirping away: So what?

I find myself drawn to a position that says, "You are quite right in all you say, but how is it helping you? Is it enough to be right? Or is there some other goal that might serve you better?" If blaming brings satisfaction, it seems a rather cold satisfaction at best. That is especially true when we consider that probably the only person we can blame who will agree with us is our own self!

I suggest we learn from Dorothy's example. I'm reasonably sure she has never read Erich Fromm, a great psychologist of the mid-20th century. But she sure appears to grasp his idea that taking responsibility means avoiding thinking in terms of what is fair—which leads to expecting an equal exchange in relationships and also to apportioning blame—and instead accepting the measure of one's own personal ability to respond to life. When Dorothy takes responsibility she acts upon her ability to respond creatively and competently to life's challenges. Being responsible, Fromm reminds is, is volunteering to respond. It isn't a duty imposed by others but a choice we make. For Dorothy the right choice is to forego blame and undertake what is within her own power—starting on the path to home. Her response is responsible.

To Forgive, Or Not to Forgive

This different way of looking at responsibility as 'response-ability' may suggest something about forgiveness. Interestingly, in Dorothy's story the issue of forgiveness is never explicit, and I suppose even as an implicit matter it is not very prominent. Her actions do suggest an ability to let go of things that holding onto would mean carrying unneeded weight. In that sense, Dorothy shows the capacity to forgive, which is one way of letting go. But let us leave Dorothy aside a moment and think this matter through ourselves in terms of our own experiences.

I cannot think of another topic more controversial in the whole arena of sexual abuse survivor issues. Some therapists and abuse survivors are sharply divided over the question of whether forgiveness of the abuser is necessary or desirable. I do detect a consensus with regard to one pivotal matter: respect for the individual survivor's own value system in settling the matter. In this matter, as in all others, the ultimate judgment belongs to each individual. To make that judgment the best possible means being clear about what forgiveness is and represents.

I already have suggested forgiveness is a form of letting go. What do we let go of? Perhaps it is the blame we want to place on ourselves or on others. Perhaps it is the anger that we have not yet experienced and eats at us like a cancer. Whatever it is we let go, the movement of forgiveness turns it into a *gift*.

That last idea is crucial. A gift is not a gift if it is mandated either by social convention or personal conscience. If I forgive because to not forgive means I feel guilty, then how is my forgiveness genuine? Forgiveness must be an outcome of a genuine movement of self toward wholeness. Then it can be an outreach of reconciliation, or perhaps even restoration. At the very least, it is a gracious letting go of the burden of thoughts, feelings, and behaviors connected to the other person that have held us back and weighed us down. In my understanding, forgiveness is neither genuine nor appropriate without it being *freely* rendered.

This point is so important it bears repeating: genuine forgiveness cannot be coerced. If we 'forgive' because we feel pressure to do so, the act itself is empty and the consequences to ourselves significantly harmful. Counselors may point out the benefits of forgiving—and there are some—but a gift given before its time is ill-given. In fact, too easily such an act can become a way of avoiding working through anxiety and pain. It may seem easier to 'just let it go' and 'forgive.' But let us not confuse passivity and a desire to escape with grace and growth.

Forgiveness is not capitulation. Forgiveness does not excuse wrongful behavior, ignore disrespect, nor promise a blissful forgetfulness. It is an act of grace that retains full memory of injustice but lets go the blame. Forgiveness defers judgment to others to make. Forgiveness chooses setting the self free over holding the perpetrator in chains of blame and loathing. It does not require feeling anything in particular; in fact, forgiveness may mean letting go of feelings. What forgiveness intends is *freedom* from the power that blame retains for the perpetrator over us. The freedom moves us away from the perpetrator and in a direction we want to go.

What forgiveness is *not* is a setting aside of wrong. It does not excuse the act or the actor who abused us. An accounting must be made, even if we are not the ones to pass judgment. Nor does forgiveness pretend that what is past is gone. Rather it resolves to keep the power of the abuse in the past rather than in the present. Finally, forgiveness does not return us to the dominion of the abuser, as in domestic violence where the survivor resubmits to the presence and power of the abuser. That act is not forgiveness but capitulation.

So should we who have been wronged forgive? Perhaps from what I have said it may seem so. Genuine forgiveness can be powerful in its benefits. Yet I resist the idea that we *ought* to forgive. No gift can be mandated. To mandate forgiveness is to disrespect the empowering choices a person requires just to be in a position to choose to forgive or not. For those of us for whom it is important to act in a spiritual manner, we may profit from recognizing the need for each person to—in the words of the New Testament—'work out your own salvation in fear and trembling' (Philippians 2:12). Forgiveness, if it comes, does not take place in a vacuum, but within the context of a long, painful process of healing and growth.

Moreover, there may be benefits to *not* forgiving. Rather than keeping us tied to our abuser, we may find that a refusal to forgive affords a measure of power and control. Forgiveness belongs to *us*. It is a gift we can withhold. An abuser may desperately desire forgiveness. But forgiveness is not an entitlement. It is not earned, it is not required, and it is not theirs to expect or demand. If refusing to forgive helps empower us, grants us a degree of control, or otherwise advantages us, it is not wrong to place our need ahead of someone else's desire.

Some of us not only find it impossible to forgive our abusers, but also to forgive God. What kind of God, especially a 'loving Father,' lets his children be abused? Or if such a God permits evil, how can he not act swiftly to bring the evil one to justice? And if justice must be deferred, why not at the very least offer comfort and healing to the victim? Some of us have spent lives in pursuit of a God of salvation who never delivers *us*.

For some of us, though, this way of looking at things may pose a dilemma. Isn't a choice not to forgive at the same time a choice to blame? The two appear inextricably intertwined. But the one choice is clearly discrete from the other. If I choose not to say the Pledge of Allegiance I am not thereby also choosing to burn the flag. The one choice does not necessitate the other. If I choose not to forgive an abuser this choice does not require I become caught up in blaming the abuser. If I do choose to forgive, then I must still resolve and resist the issues of blaming. Or to put it in a more sensible order, I best serve myself by resolving the blame issues before considering the question of forgiveness.

I cannot speak for anyone other than myself, but I will certainly try to make my own understanding plain. I reject unequivocally the idea that to choose not to forgive is an inauthentic or inferior choice. In many instances it is the only authentic, mature, and responsible choice. Only we who have the gift can decide whether to give it, to whom, or when.

However, I do urge all of us who have survived abuse to forgive ourselves. That may seem an incredible thing to say since survivors are emphatically *not* responsible for the wrongs done to us. But it remains a fact that we survivors commonly struggle with self-blame, with guilt and a sense that in some manner we caused what happened. It is rarely enough to just tell one's self that "It isn't my fault." A formal declaration of forgiveness may be needed. I even encourage that this declaration be made into as beautiful and rich a religious ritual as we can find or devise. A survivor merits such a gift.

Learning the Hard Way

Maybe most of us are like my friend Dorothy. We struggle with fear, self-blame, and a sinking conviction that we are at the center, not of the world, but of a cesspool. With Auntie Em, Dorothy was emphatic that she was the one to blame for any trouble her dog had caused. Later, fearful of little Toto again being taken by the shrewish Miss Gulch, Dorothy and Toto set off down the dusty road in front of the farm. Dorothy is off looking for rescue and a place of safety. Of course, when she meets Professor Marvel, who gazes into his crystal ball and reminds her of Auntie Em with the careworn face and saddened heart, then Dorothy immediately turns back toward home. But before she can be reunited with her Aunt and Uncle she must pass through Oz on the yellow brick road.

Yes, Dorothy *must* walk the yellow brick road, even if—strictly speaking—it was not necessary for her to do so to get home. So why does she have to walk the yellow brick road? Consider: after walking the length and breadth of Oz—literally from East to West—and slaying two wicked witches, gaining honor and steadfast friends in the process, Dorothy at last learns that the power to be home in Kansas has been in her all along. Glinda, the good witch of the North, has known this from the beginning but has said nothing. Now, when Dorothy learns this knowledge has been withheld from her, who could blame her if she stoops, grabs a brick and sends it sailing at Glinda's head? I can hear myself crying out, "What do you mean I could have gone home anytime—and you knew it all the time?! You sent me to risk my neck when it was unnecessary?! And you call yourself a *good* witch?!"

Perhaps these thoughts actually pass through Dorothy's mind before Glinda explains herself. Be that as it may, Glinda's answer apparently makes sense to Dorothy. "You would not have believed me had I told you." The realization that Dorothy had this power within her that would make the magic of the ruby slippers obey her wish is something she has to find out for herself. But that means walking dusty roads in Kansas and yellow brick ones in Oz.

A Latin expression says *experientia docet*. Experience teaches. Dorothy requires the experiences of Oz to realize her own capabilities. The point is not that Dorothy is a dolt for needing this kind of instruction, nor that she is a slow learner for having to take so much time and undergo such hard times to acquire it. The point is: Dorothy learns.

And that does not happen while she spends her time sitting in blame and hurling bricks; it happens while walking the road.

Chapter 3

HOW LESSONS ARE LEARNED
IN KANSAS AND IN OZ

Lessons

Questions loom, storm clouds darkening the evening sky:
        How many of me are there?
        Where do I begin and where do I end?
        What did I do to bring this upon me?
        Why? Why? Why? Why? Why?

Acid rain falls burningly; in drops, the scalding cry:
        You are Legion, a demon's lair!
        You are timeless in a sin without mend!
        You are the bitter of the dead salt sea!
        Die! Die! Die! Die! Die!

But Dorothy's dreaming voice sweetly lights the sky:
        Somewhere over the rainbow I can dare
        to walk yellow brick roads round every bend,
        to gather my waters in purity.
        I . . . I . . . I . . . I . . . I

am on song wings, rounding the rainbow to Oz!

Learning

Just what does Dorothy have to learn—and how? Why is walking through Oz so important? Last chapter we teased with the answer at the end: *experience teaches*. But the suggestion raised there is so important we need to give it substantial time and very careful consideration. I think what we will find will prove the key to understanding why the big lesson of life and of Oz first mentioned in chapter one is truly that, the BIG lesson.

Let's begin with some quick, clear answers to some important questions and then take a more leisurely stroll through the reasoning behind them. First, what does Dorothy have to learn? As mentioned in the first chapter, she must learn that she all along possesses the ability to be where she wants to be. But before she can learn that larger lesson she has to master a number of essential smaller ones. While this whole book is mostly about the big lesson—learning by experience what we are capable of in reaching where we want to be—the different chapters tackle one or another of the other essential lessons as well. For instance, in this chapter we will examine *how* these lessons are learned. Why is walking through Oz so important? The walking of the yellow brick road gives times and experiences to Dorothy that change her and make her ready to realize the answers and power that is within her the whole time. Walking liberates what has been bound up inside.

Our Bodies, Our Tablets

How does Dorothy learn, then? She learns like we all do, through experience. She learns by walking rather than sitting. She learns by avoiding blame and taking responsibility. But the key ingredient for Dorothy and for us is our *bodies*. Our bodies are the tablets on which the lessons of life are written. All experiences affect our body and all lessons begin there.

Experience is how our bodies navigate the world. Everything outside comes into us through our bodies, lodges in our bodies, is felt, translated, thought about, and acted upon by our bodies. Let's allegorize a minute. The body is like a sailing ship. As we plow through life's waters, varying weather conditions and currents (i.e., things in the environment) indicate how the sails should be placed, or trimmed, or unfurled. The size and strength of the ship (i.e., age and constitutional makeup) set boundaries to what the ship can and cannot manage. The feel of the ship, the way her timbers shudder in the wind or how her prow slices the waves (i.e., sensations and emotions), caution or encourage the crew to undertake certain acts (i.e., behaviors). The captain (i.e., the mind) calls out orders to guide the ship, turning it this direction or that. Hopefully, the ship is sailing purposefully rather than merely reacting to the seas. But even the captain with the firmest plan still is a lousy skipper if he or she does not consult the currents or winds, the capabilities of the ship, and its current condition.

Nobody sails without a vessel. Apart from the body there is no experience from which to learn. Dorothy is no different than any of the rest of us in respect of having to experience in order to learn and having to have a body in order to experience. At the same time, like each of us, Dorothy is absolutely unique and irreplaceable. Her experiences, like her body, are uniquely her own. No one can have them for her.

The violation represented by sexual abuse affects us the way it does because it so directly and blatantly offends the tablet of our experience. No wonder our subsequent experiences seem so marked by what has been traced on the tablet of our body. By violating our bodies, our experiences are twisted, perverted, and stolen as though they—and our bodies—actually belong to those who abuse us. Sexual violations are lies enacted against us that seek to steal the truth of our bodies and our experiences. Recovery from abuse is reclaiming the truth that our bodies are our own and that our experiences are too.

I find it interesting that part of being unique is learning different lessons at different speeds in different ways. Since everybody is a different body, too, it certainly does not seem awry to me to suggest that everything about our learning from experience is rooted in our being different bodies. Of course, I don't intend to develop some kind of far-fetched scheme that purports to tell people what kind of body type is best suited to learn what kind of lessons. The matter is far different from that. Our bodies are much more than our skin or individual shape. For instance, we are as different *inside* in the way our brains' fine connections form to make individual, continually changing patterns as we are outwardly in our unique fingerprints. It is not just genetics that account for these differences between individuals; experience counts significantly. Through experience our brains are modified; we call relatively permanent changes due to experience 'learning.' It is partly the scadzillion little ways our brain cells orchestrate to sing to one another that make our insides so uniquely us and our learning so definitely personal.

My point is that each of us learns in accordance with the way we are put together inside our bodies. At the same time, the way we are wired in our body is shaped by our bodily experience of the world. If this sounds circular, it is. Human existence is the ceaseless interaction between ourselves (and our selves are our bodies) and the world, with each constantly making changes, tiny or large, in the other. In a sense, our learning and its products are the sum of all these changes.

Dorothy, too, is unique. The experiences of her short lifetime bring her to where she is in Oz when the first foot is placed on the yellow brick road. Every step brings changes in Dorothy and in Oz alike. Who can argue that Oz is not profoundly altered by this little Kansan girl? But our concern remains with how Dorothy grows. Telling of how Oz is changed is another story.

Glinda does not hint that Dorothy is a slow learner or even that she might be resistant to instruction. But she avoids telling Dorothy something she isn't ready to hear because Glinda knows Dorothy has to learn some things in her body and across time before she can realize them in her mind. As for her mind itself, perspective relies on insight, but gaining insight is not a linear process. Insight comes in surprising flashes and hard won truths as we traverse a winding trail. Apart from the time spent walking throughout Oz, Dorothy cannot fire the experiences necessary to forge words.

Glinda is not only a good witch; she is a wise one. Already in Oz she knows something we in Kansas have been slow to accept as true. *All* learning and memory are rooted in the body. Unless an idea takes root in our body and extends itself through the sensations of our experience, it will never sustain itself. For that matter, no idea can register without being the seed of some experience, no matter how trivial or unnoticed. But the really major ideas, those that grip our mind and guide our feelings, are those whose impact upon our body is most pronounced. It is not the thought of wicked witches that impresses Dorothy most, but the witch's locking her alone in a castle's tower room that sends her into despair. Experience teaches us precisely because it happens to, and in, our bodies and alters them.

Let's ask it again: what exactly does Dorothy learn? When asked that question by Tin Woodsman, she answers to Glinda and her companions that she now knows it is not enough to want something. Merely wishing to see Auntie Em and Uncle Henry is insufficient. The next time she sets out to search for what is important, what she terms her heart's desire, Dorothy says she will look no further than her own backyard, "for if it isn't there, then I never really lost it." I think we can metaphorically understand that as meaning she need look no further than herself. What she is looking for resides within her, not outside her, or—in terms Dorothy can embrace—the answer is in Kansas, not in Oz.

A Two-edged Sword

Experience is a two-edged sword both in Kansas and in Oz. Experience has the power to shape us in healthy, self-fulfilling directions, or to lock us into self-destructive patterns. The more powerful the experience, the more changes it may produce. An experience that shows Dorothy that Oz is a relatively benign and safe kingdom, such as the happy encounter with Scarecrow, elicits from her hope, confidence and enthusiasm. But being trapped alone in the witch's tower, watching her Auntie Em call longingly for her through the crystal ball while being unable to be heard in return, elicits fear and despair. Dorothy lives these experiences in her body. Her body undergoes changes as she has these experiences. And she is a different person by virtue of them.

In a moment, we shall investigate more closely the nature of the changes that occur in our bodies when they are exposed to a trauma such as sexual abuse. It is important to do so because too many of us have been told that our experience was insignificant or unreal. The sexual violation of our bodies is generally treated as just a psychological problem within our minds, as though what happened in the body doesn't really matter. But it *does* matter and we should understand why.

First, though, I want to highlight a little longer this contrast between healthy and hurtful experiences. To facilitate the former I am advocating the use of metaphor as a way of counterbalancing the wounding effect of the latter kind of experience. We can imaginatively experience metaphors and stories in our bodies in ways that help heal them of the hurt visited in the world. In short, we can use Oz to help us handle Kansas. What I am proposing, actually, is following what we see Dorothy doing in Oz.

Dorothy is a nicely balanced person. Instead of being overwhelmed by the possible disasters that hang over her head in a strange place she takes positive steps and builds a store of resources to help her succeed in the face of different challenges. On the other hand, she avoids a Pollyanna optimism that ignores her very real peril. Dorothy knows how and when to be afraid. But she does not collapse, because she has resources to draw upon to keep her balance.

Dorothy isn't a bad therapist, either. When she meets Scarecrow, he bemoans his inability to scare the crows of Oz. Dorothy, in reassuring him that any Scarecrow such as himself would be a spectacular success in Kansas, lends him a new, competing image. Having a new way to look at his own person and actions, one that says he would be a success in a different environment, immediately raises Scarecrow's self-esteem. It also changes his perception of the environment by broadening it. Oz is not the only reality; in Kansas he can be more than his experience in Oz has indicated.

Now Scarecrow has not actually experienced Kansas. But Dorothy grants him the experience imaginatively and its effect upon him is as real *as if* he had himself been there. Scarecrow's investment of trust and belief in Dorothy is sufficient magic to put him in Kansas without ever being there, so to speak, 'in the straw.' His metaphorical experience has an effect on his body that counterbalances his so-called 'real' experiences in Oz. What is real is how his ability to imagine being different helps him *be* different. He is what he can imagine.

The Wizard of Oz is even more a master of the power of metaphor in rewarding Scarecrow, Tin Woodsman, and Lion. The ritual granting of symbols for what the three companions already possess is a metaphorical experience that makes concrete what they previously had no insight about. Each is changed. Each sees himself in a new, healthier way. Building on real experiences in Oz, the wizard helps each grasp the reality that is inside them by using metaphorical magic in the power of ritual and symbol. In this fashion, the wizard counterbalances—in fact, overbalances—the previous experiences that had suggested falsely to each that he was without brains, or a heart, or courage.

Perhaps the above illustrates why metaphors are so crucial. Metaphors often suggest themselves from our own experience—experience rooted in and mediated by our bodies. For many of us, as survivors of sexual abuse, life's circumstances lend themselves more readily to negative messages about who we are and what we are capable of attaining or being. Experience seems to have taught us we are never good enough, or that we are deficient, or that we are simply terrible persons. We adopt distorted images reflecting our body's altered awareness. We may see ourselves as fat when we are dangerously underweight. We use metaphors that reinforce to ourselves the cruel lessons of the abuse. Some of us who accepted gifts in connection with the abuse might come to view ourselves as whores—and one day literally enflesh that metaphor on the streets.

Lessons are more than 'just in our head.' Or, more accurately, they are *literally* in our head, in the real physical changes that take place in how our brain cells relate to each other and in the chemical messengers they use to accomplish that. From these minute changes snowball a sequence that can reach the proportions of an avalanche.

Experience is a two-edged sword poised above our bodies, twirling slowly on a gossamer strand. It can sever life from us, or wound us deeply, or cut away the cancerous false starts we may have made. But the drama is not played out on the blade's surface. It is enacted in our bodies, the tablets that record our life experiences. Our bodies are also the vehicles in which we move through life. Or, looked at a little differently, the body is itself the road our experiences walk. Depending on the experience, our bodies may be paths toward health or disease, life or death.

How can we not seek out transformative metaphors when we realize that our bodies are crossroads in Oz waiting to be walked either to the Emerald City or the wicked witch's castle?

Traumatic Lessons in the Body

None of the changes Dorothy undergoes is more profound than the one that translates her from Kansas to Oz. But then, if a tornado is not an experience that alters a person, then Kansas isn't flat! Those who experience sexual abuse are changed, too. One of the challenges facing those of us who work with survivors of sexual abuse is finding ways to communicate the reality and nature of the changes wrought by the tornado of abuse. Counselors are right to think that it is important for clients to understand what has happened in body and mind. In psychology the changes we encounter because of our experience are collectively termed the 'psychobiology of abuse trauma,' which is a shorthand manner of saying that the ways we feel, think, and act after surviving a wounding event are rooted in bodily changes. Counselors can help us see how the potentially lethal threat of sexual abuse powerfully alters our body chemistry. The stress hormone adrenalin (also called epinephrine) prepares us to flee or fight, if we can. But for each of us the exact pattern of change and response is unique.

Still, while everyone's body (i.e., each self) is different, and everyone responds to trauma individually, this fact can be exaggerated. Being human means sharing a basic kind of anatomy and physiology that sets limits to how different individual variability can be. Experts tell us that our central nervous system has definite constraints on it that set us along a rather consistent response path. In other words, despite individual variability, there is a recognizable constellation of changes and effects associated with sexual abuse. We are not completely alone in how this experience has affected us—and that is good news.

To describe these effects we will need to consider minute changes in the body that eventuate in large changes in behavior. I recognize that trying to describe these changes will take many of us into foreign territory, where the language is strange, perhaps incomprehensible. But if patience and persistence is needed to figure out the land, the journey is well worth it, for this is a place every survivor of sexual abuse has visited. We can profit from understanding it clearly. Then we can give answer to the ignorance surrounding us in the words even doctors often give in not understanding what we have survived.

In the remainder of this chapter I will try to explain how our bodies learn from experience by undergoing changes at microscopic levels. The kind of changes that neuroscientists suggest be described to abuse survivors will be the subject of the next chapter. In order to understand those larger bodily changes we must first see how the body learns life's lessons. Then we will be in a position to view how terrible the effects can be when the lessons learned are the sorrowful ones of abuse.

Let's begin with an important clarification. We have been considering that the experiences that affect our bodies come from our environments. I want to clarify that our environments can be either internal or external. We are most often accustomed to thinking of an environment as something outside of us— the room we are in, or the city, for example. However, we each have an internal environment as well. Some of the major parts of that environment are physical organs, like the brain, heart, lungs, and liver, while others are psychological realities flowing from and rooted in our body parts and what they experience.

Some parts of our inner environment are incredibly small, like the tiny chemicals that tell our organs to do this or that. Our internal environment seeks a kind of even-tempered state we call *homeostasis,* where the body very naturally maintains healthy, appropriate levels for many functions, such as our heartbeat, blood pressure, body temperature, and balance of secretions by our various hormonal glands. For any number of reasons, our internal environment often has this delicate homeostatic balance upset. When that happens both smaller and larger changes take place. In this chapter we are concerned with the smaller changes that underlie the larger ones considered in the next chapter. To put it another way, in this chapter we are looking at how our body learns; next chapter we view the application of the lessons.

Now back to the idea of environments. Our internal and external environments interact. To give an obvious example, if we eat something disagreeable, such as a spoiled fish at a restaurant, our external environment will have impacted our internal environment so as to create an upset. If that upset leads to our vomiting dinner all over the restaurant's table and floor, it is safe to say we will have influenced the external environment as well. The ceaseless flow of transactions between the internal and external environments through our bodies, where these environments meet, is a wondrous process that merits being celebrated and safeguarded so that both external and internal environments prosper.

One particular aspect of environment needs to be singled out because of its significance for sexual abuse. Those who study the human brain tell us that our brain cells are influenced by our environment, especially by the behavior of other people. What others say and do affects the very makeup of our brain— how cells organize and talk to each other. And that changes how we may think, feel, and act.

Imagine that! What Glinda and the wicked witch alike accomplish is to alter how Dorothy's brain cells function! Obviously, other human beings are very important parts of our external environments. Other human beings have a major role in changing our internal environments.

When sexual abuse occurs, one or more persons, acting as perpetrators of a trauma (the word means 'wound'), alter the brain functioning of the victim (and, incidentally, their own). Fortunately, our brain and the rest of our body possesses a remarkable flexibility which psychobiologists call *plasticity*. The term refers to the ability of the brain's nerve cells to mold themselves into new networking forms in order to increase the chances of successfully managing a changing environment. Biologically, it is this neural plasticity—our brain cells' ability to shift how they relate to each other—that underlies new learning and, ultimately, the new behaviors we have to use to cope in the environment. In short, our body's ability to alter itself in the face of environmental information is an adaptation possessing the quality of change in order to keep us alive.

Some of us are better than others at adaptation. A word used to reflect this reality is *resiliency*. This is the degree of a person's ability to jump back into life, to get back on the horse when bucked off, to become buoyant again after having been deflated by a circumstance. It is also the quality of flexibility by which someone adjusts to the new and unexpected.

Please don't confuse resiliency with *denial*, where a person acts as if nothing has happened, or—more commonly—*minimizes* the severity of what has occurred. In extreme denial a person may bury an event or series of events so thoroughly that they can gain conscious awareness again only at great cost. This is what psychologists and psychiatrists mean by the word *repression*. Resiliency is something different. With the unknown or unfamiliar, it finds a way to accommodate the strangeness so as not to become overly stuck. With life's wounds it is realistic, acknowledging the hurt but finding a way to integrate it into the whole fabric of life so that healthy living can proceed. Please remember, too, that even resilient people require time to recover from duress.

Dorothy is resilient. When we watch her walking the yellow brick road, we are aware of her growing degree of comfort. All the oddities of Oz that amaze her in Munchkin Land become accepted as part of her expected world by the time she reaches the Emerald City with the wicked witch's broom. Although we cannot peel back her cranium to microscopically examine the changes in her brain, we can be sure they are occurring because Dorothy adapts to Oz. Neural plasticity—this phenomena of our brain's intricate map of nerve cell connections and communications constantly, subtly shifting to help us cope—may remain invisible at one level, but its effects in our behavior are plain enough.

The marvel of life is that changes at the tiniest microscopic level can and do play out on a much larger level. Clearly, not all changes are equal. Some changes at this smallest level are short-lived. They occur, but they don't persist. However, even small changes can have ripple effects that endure long past the event that started them. Long-term changes are especially interesting because they have so many repercussions for the quality of our life and relationships. As changes persist they can be expected to show up in those enduring patterns of behavior that we think of as an individual's personality.

In fact, some neuroscientists describe personality as consisting of many diverse processes, collectively sensitive to changes prompted by our environment, although typically in subtle ways. These sensitive processes function at a microscopic level and create varying degrees of impact on the whole person. This is why personality can be relatively stable and persistent while still possessing a wide range of minor changes and fluctuations. Dorothy certainly is a different young woman by the end of the yellow brick road, but she remains Dorothy. The native innocence, childlike wonder, heartfelt compassion, and simple gumption that characterize her in Munchkin Land are still there in the Emerald City. While adapting to Oz, Dorothy not only remains true to herself, she changes in the direction of becoming *more* herself. The neural processes involved within her are continually altering to reflect her adaptation to the environment of Oz.

These personality-altering processes are pursued through the kind of systems, or networks, of nerve cells that make up what a neuroscientist might call a 'module,' which is a basic neural functioning unit. In other words, what makes Dorothy who she is—and makes us who we are—is shaped by many interacting groups of nerve cells. Each group, or module, can be viewed as one unit, with connections inside itself and between itself and other modules. At the risk of being overly simplistic, think of the brain as a set of Leggo toy pieces. These can be joined together to form various units, say a block here and a tower there, and then the units joined to form a walled city. Personality is made up of smaller identifiable units that are joined to form a larger matrix.

A neuroscientist might tell us that human adaptation requires the effective working of a variety of modules responsible for mediating many facets of human existence. Think a moment of the kinds of things involved in our living in the world, each of them requiring mental effort: sensing and perceiving our environment, selecting what we need to live in it, motivating ourselves to get it, and doing all of these things while in complex relationships with others. What happens at the level of our individual brain cells is marvelously coordinated to create purposeful behavior.

Obviously, if the environment adversely affects the functioning of modules, then disastrous consequences may result for one or more of these important functions. For example, the quality of attachment between the affected person and significant others may be profoundly damaged. Or, the regulating of the sexual and aggressive impulses may be weakened so that others or the self are injured by inappropriate behaviors. It is like our Leggo city having a breach in the walls where some pieces have been smashed or removed. But the consequences for a person are far more serious than the spoiling of a child's play set.

From what might at first seem little, subtle changes in neural configurations—the modules behind personality—come the substantial effects of a changed person. This is why neuropsychologists can claim that neural plasticity matters for personality theory. Built, as it were, from the ground floor up, the changes in tiny brain cells can add up to relatively enduring changes in personality after traumas like sexual abuse. As I suggested earlier, the more intense the experience, the more impact it is likely to have. Few things we encounter in life may be more intense than sexual abuse. It is hardly a stretch to see it profoundly altering our brains in ways that ultimately affect personality.

If I can put this in more everyday terms, what they are saying is that the wounds of something like sexual abuse can arise from intensely experienced and felt events. These intense events penetrate deeply into our body, like a massive jolt that rewires our brains. As our brains settle into their new patterns— patterns designed to help survival—the new ways of thinking, feeling, and acting that were brought about by the abuse become habits. These habits persist even into the posttraumatic phase, that is, the time when the abuse has stopped externally but we still act internally as though it is continuing. As a result, the very skills we found useful for keeping us alive during the abuse now get in our way when the externally abusive environment is gone.

Can you imagine Dorothy on her return to Kansas acting like she had in Oz? In Oz it is adaptive to believe Scarecrows have brains, talk and dance, and make wonderful friends. In Kansas this belief can get one locked away. Or, if Dorothy acts in Oz like she might in Kansas, then the wicked witch is probably ignored and Dorothy ends up dead. The measure of Dorothy's health is that she adapts appropriately to these dramatically different environments.

For anyone who doubts the consequences of trying to bring Oz back to Kansas, consider the reaction that Dorothy gets from Auntie Em, Uncle Henry, Professor Marvel, and the farmhands gathered at her bedside when she finds herself back in Kansas. They chuckle when she tries to relate even the fragments of her story, and Auntie Em assures her "we all dream silly things." Her Uncle Henry's assurance that Dorothy is believed is understandable only as the relief and affection shown in finding a loved one is going to be okay.

But Dorothy can only stay okay by planting her feet again on Kansan roads and leaving the yellow brick road of Oz.

A Summary

Learning, we see, comes by experience, and experience depends on the body. Body changes are the biology of learning. Whether we are Dorothy in Oz, or sexual abuse survivors, we all learn and remember by the same mechanisms. Our brains are shaped by our experiences. Our brains undergo subtle changes in order to facilitate our adaptation to ever changing environments. The more intense or prolonged the experience, the more profound the bodily lesson may be. Sexual abuse can prove a very intense experience that initiates changes that may dramatically alter a person's very personality. But because our brains are able to change, we may hope in the power of significant metaphorical experiences to counterbalance the unhealthy changes induced by abuse. Like Dorothy in Oz, we can learn new ways of being to get where we want to be. In some very important ways we *can* go home again.

Chapter 4

THE SCARECROW'S LESSON

The Witch's Guard

Racing . . . hurry, hurry . . . oh, faster Toto!
After us . . . always, always . . . after us!

My heart . . . exploding . . . but oh, oh, oh!
Monkey hands . . . wings . . . hurt because

Oh Toto! . . . I'm frightened . . . Auntie Em!
Uncle Henry! . . . sky above so dark

Toto, where are you?
ground below so stark

I'm frightened by them.

Any . . . rescue?

Body, Body. . . Who's Got a Body?

Dorothy is hardly alone along the steep learning curve that is Oz. Her companions all have lessons to learn as well. There are brains to be used, a heart to be broken, and courage to be proved. Like their beloved Dorothy, Scarecrow, Tin Woodsman, and Cowardly Lion have bodies impacted by experience. A pivotal one comes along the road to find the wicked witch of the West. The witch's winged monkeys ambush the band of friends.

Suddenly, Dorothy is gone and her companions must fend for themselves. We shall return to Dorothy in due time, but in this chapter we shall linger behind with her friends in those first awful moments after Dorothy has been snatched away. It is a time when the loyal Scarecrow suddenly finds himself with more to worry about than whether he will ever have a brain. As the wicked witch's minions, the flying monkeys, capture Dorothy and Toto, Scarecrow is ripped apart. Suddenly, for Scarecrow the most immediate issue is whether he will ever again have a body.

We all should be able to relate to Scarecrow's worry. Periodically life seems to remind us that living depends on having a body. Last chapter we mused together about one important aspect of our having bodies, namely that all learning depends on bodily experience and involves bodily changes. But like Scarecrow, we have been preoccupied with the brain. We have spent time trying to understand how the brain physically changes to make learning happen and what that may mean for those of us who have endured sexual abuse.

Now the witch's monkeys are upon us and we are forcefully reminded that brains do not exist in isolation. Apart from the rest of the straw we are going to go nowhere. Fortunately, Scarecrow realizes that he needs his stuffing. He tells the Cowardly Lion and the Tin Woodsman that the monkeys have torn off his legs and tossed his chest straw in the opposite direction. Rightly Tin Woodsman, surveying the scattered damage, remarks, "That's you all over!" Rightly, too, Lion comments the monkeys have knocked the stuffing out of his friend. However, Scarecrow is rightest of all. He knows he must be put together again if Dorothy is to be rescued.

Let's weigh all three responses to Scarecrow's trauma. Tin Woodsman focuses on the effects of the attack and accurately sums up in a way I might paraphrase as, "Boy, are you a mess!" Lion focuses upon the attack itself, which quite literally took the stuffing right out of the Scarecrow. Both are absolutely right in their observations and yet both completely miss the point that Scarecrow at once seizes upon—but then, he's the one with the brains! He sees the issue that matters most lies in the present and in the immediate future, not in the past. He must get himself put back together bodily before he can accomplish what he wants to accomplish.

All three clearly see that the Scarecrow's body is at the heart of the problem, no matter how the problem is assessed.

The Cowardly Lion's Perspective

"They sure knocked the stuffing out of you, didn't they?"

Lion's question to Scarecrow might be asked of any of us at one time or another. However, we are more likely to mean it figuratively though Lion's literal meaning is the better one. Trauma does more than take the wind out of our sails; it rends the fabric in ugly gashes. Before the sail can be put to useful work again it is imperative that the damage be accurately appraised. That appraisal is Lion's immediate contribution to Scarecrow's problematic situation.

So let us spend some time seeing how the stuffing in us is affected by trauma. Last chapter we talked about the effect in connection with learning and experience. Now we can be specific about exactly how the lessons are applied in the body. To put that in perspective, though, requires we start with a brief look at human evolution. Our bodies are the way they are today because of millennia of success in a world far less comfortable than our own.

In the grand scale of time it has not been that long since we human beings were scurrying about the forest trying to keep our hides intact from various threatening predators. Our bodies were equipped with a number of useful biological systems that aided our adaptation to a world filled with lurking beasts in the shadows. We had early warning systems that went off when we approached dangerous situations. We had rapid response systems that appraised environmental stimuli like a crouching bear and told us whether to run or stand our ground. We had mobilization responses that shut down certain body functions, such as digestion, for a time while the energy was shifted to other body functions, like increased oxygen to muscles that might be needed in fleeing or fighting. In short, we proved a successful species in an often physically hostile environment because our bodies were wired to cope with physical threats.

Time and technological progress has eased for most of us the likelihood of being chased through the jungle by a tiger. But our bodies have not kept pace with our technology. Instead, our bodies have made uneasy compromises with the social and technological changes of human history. In addition to clicking on when we are faced by muggers in the city jungle, our body systems operate whenever anything in our social world suggests a threat to our well-being. Adaptation has not meant setting aside the systems we relied on for physical safety in a bygone era, but extending them to cover a whole range of new threats that life on the savannah never imagined.

For we human beings what appears to have happened is this: as we developed greater independence from the physical environment and its natural menaces, we simultaneously became more dependent on our psychosocial environment. In short, we have developed into beings whose greatest stress and risk of harm comes from one another. Our bodies have responded to the shift from a dependence on the physical environment to greater dependence on the psychosocial environment by utilizing the same resources for *social* threats that always have been used for *physical* threats. So nowadays our big challenge is how to adapt to the emotional and relational challenges posed by other people.

When something such as sexual abuse occurs a number of factors enter. First, there is the actual physical component of the sexual contact. This may or may not be experienced as painful, but it remains intrusive. Second, there is the social component, which disapproves of such physical contact. Third, there is the psychological component, which may interpret the physical and social factors in any number of ways. Add these together and stir well in the body and the result is a boiling chemical soup inside us that is more likely than not to create problems for some time to come.

Without trying to be too detailed concerning the ingredients or how the soup is stirred, some general discussion of what is going on inside the body seems in order. Unlike Scarecrow, whose biology is straw, human workings are a bit more complicated. But no less than Scarecrow, we also can have the stuffing kicked out of us. To understand this happening means acquiring some sense of how our bodies respond to sexual abuse *as if* it were a ferocious bear or ravenous tiger.

Let's follow the order suggested by Scarecrow's report. First he said, "they tore my legs off and they threw them over there!" Scarecrow begins with his body's outer boundaries. Trauma works its way from the outside in, like a worm into an apple. We incorporate—a metaphorical word about the body taking something into itself—the world through the portals of our senses: sight, smell, touch, hearing, and taste. In sexual abuse all of these are likely to be significantly involved.

Our senses translate and convey this information to the interior parts of our body along nerves and through chemical messengers that relay signals from one nerve to the next. The nerves under our skin and all about the boundaries of our body are called the peripheral nervous system (PNS). In terms of its function, this system has two major divisions, one responsible for taking sensory information to the central nervous system (CNS) and the other for putting the CNS's commands to work. Our eyes, for example, send what they see in a chemically coded form to the CNS. Our brains interpret the sensory information and send directions to the appropriate body parts. If what our eyes are seeing is a ball flying toward our face, the brain's message will be "Duck!"

"Then they took my chest out, and they threw it over there!" said Scarecrow. After the outer body boundaries the more central body regions are affected. Let's follow our example of the ball zinging at us. The message which adds up to the one word "Duck!" is actually made up of many parts. The PNS, through its first (i.e., sensory) division sends the image. The CNS interprets the danger and relays back a decision to the PNS through its second division (called the motor division because it moves us). The CNS also sends a signal to the endocrine system, another messenger system. The endocrine system uses hormones for its messengers, such as adrenaline (also known as epinephrine). A hormone like this one has widespread effects. Adrenaline tells the heart to beat harder and faster, which pumps blood and the oxygen it bears to places where muscles need it to respond rapidly and get us out of harm's way. Other hormones accomplish other effects that assist the nervous system in getting the body to do what it must to protect itself.

So the PNS talks to the CNS, which talks back to the PNS while also passing a warning to the endocrine system. In stressful situations, the communication centers especially shout to a part of the motor division of the PNS called the autonomic nervous system (ANS). This system also has two parts, one called the sympathetic nervous system and the other the parasympathetic (which means 'alongside the sympathetic') nervous system. The sympathetic nervous system is crucial to the body's response to stress. It orchestrates the dampening and heightening of many bodily activities, such as breathing and digesting, in order to ensure that those parts of the body most needed to cope with the emergency have the most resources at hand. The total result is that muscles are being moved, blood is being pushed along where it is needed most, and all the body's many parts are dancing in a complicated step to the hooting and hollering of the body's messenger systems.

But Scarecrow sums it up just as well when he lays on the ground, arms flailing uselessly, and cries out, "Help, help!" The trauma of sundered legs and chest, of body boundaries and internal invasion, results in a set of responses that have a single aim: the procuring of survival. Everything our body is doing at such a time is like screaming, "Help!" and then trying to answer our own voice's call.

So What?

I find what is happening in the body as it responds to stress and trauma fascinating and instructive. Still, I suppose it is only natural if at this point some of you are asking, "So what? So what that the body responds like this?" The questions are fair. After all, the body mobilizes any time there is a threat. God knows stress seems almost ubiquitous in today's world. So what's all the fuss about?

First, it is important to know that sexual abuse is not something that affects us psychologically but not physically. Balderdash! Abuse trauma wounds us mentally and emotionally *because* it affects us biologically. *Sexual abuse creates real physical changes that generate the psychological changes we experience.* Can you imagine what the scene might be like if Tin Woodsman, instead of asking Scarecrow what has happened, simply told him, "Come on, you lazy, shiftless bum! There's nothing wrong with you. Quit swinging your arms like that, get off the ground, and let's get going!" In addition to being factually incorrect, the admonitions would only add to the injury Scarecrow experiences because, instead of validating his experience, the remarks deny it and at the same time blame Scarecrow for his condition.

This isn't unlike the experience many sexual abuse survivors have with their family doctors when time or other circumstances have eroded any obvious physical markers the sexual abuse may have made—and sexual abuse does not always leave obvious physical marks anyway. We face a Western cultural bias that infects medicine all too often. This bias makes psychological problems less real than illnesses with a readily identifiable germ. All of a sudden, different values, criteria, and procedures come into play. From the moment a person enters with complaints of 'a suspiciously psychological nature,' he or she is moved into an arena of consideration different from the person who comes in complaining of a bacterially inspired stomach flu.

There is a higher social status to having a clearly discernible physical cause for distress! As a result, sexual abuse survivors often find their visits with medical doctors distressing because their complaints aren't taken as seriously as they might be if they came in complaining of an ingrown toenail. Since most of us have been taught to revere physicians, their implicit judgment affects how we see ourselves and our concerns. We may give ourselves over to an unspoken judgment that our health complaints are unjustified, or at least should not be seen as worthy of a 'real doctor.' So we get shunted off to a psychiatrist, psychologist, or counselor as someone with problems who are all 'in the head' rather than truly body-based.

What happens, then, to a person diagnosed with a psychiatric condition? She or he may be doomed to negative judgments by the 'helper' assigned to the case. Imagine Tin Woodsman, he of the yearning for a heart, as a doctor assigned to Scarecrow in our imaginary scenario. Suppose he concludes there is no organic agent responsible for Scarecrow's condition, nor any environmental trauma to be blamed. (I grant, given Scarecrow's lack of legs and a torn apart chest that I am asking a significant suspension of disbelief on this point, but bear with me.) Though the patient complains of physical distress, if it cannot be accounted for by expectable, readily observable physical causes, it may be judged to be *self*-caused. If it is self-caused, reasons Tin Woodsman, then Scarecrow must have a reason for wanting to be sick. He may, like many another physician, pencil onto the medical chart: "the secondary gains obtained from the disorder are too strong." In other words, Scarecrow does not want to get well!

But then the insult of disregarding the body basis of our psychological distress has added to it the injury of becoming a second-class citizen in the world of medical care. There is no label like being branded a 'mental patient.' That is especially true in a system of care that tends to start from the assumption that psychological problems are the person's fault. So, branded with what feels like a large scarlet 'M' for Mental on our forehead for all the world to see, we are shunted off to someone who nods sympathetically while telling us that our problems are just in our head. And that may feel like being told they aren't *real.*

Or, as Tin Woodsman in our little play might say, "Come on, Scarecrow—get a grip on yourself!" That may be what we hear. But merely because the changes wrought by sexual abuse are elusive to the medical eye does not mean that the mental, emotional, and behavioral problems are somehow nonbiological. The realization that abuse trauma is rooted in biological changes is absolutely essential for a survivor's sense of self-esteem in a culture where the only health problems recognized as real are ones understood as biological in nature.

This first realization will lead to others no less important. But we will consider just one more reason why all the time we are spending on this question is appropriate. This second reason will then provide a springboard for the next level of reflection about Scarecrow's condition. Sexual abuse can change our biological patterns so as to keep our emotional and mental condition chaotic for a long time, with the result that our behaviors become less and less adaptive.

Suppose Scarecrow believes what Tin Woodsman in our imaginary situation has just told him. He thinks to himself, "Perhaps he's right. Maybe I'm only imagining that I was just torn apart by chittering, flying monkeys. I feel like I'm scattered into a million pieces, but he says nothing is wrong with me, so I must at least be exaggerating." So Scarecrow rolls himself over and starts crawling along the ground with his arms. All the while, naturally, Tin Woodsman is likely to be carrying on his criticism. "I just don't understand you, Scarecrow. You're getting slower every day. Why can't you keep up with us? And how come every time I ask you to hand me something you come to a complete stop?"

Just how adaptive do you suppose Scarecrow's behavior is going to be as the days wear on?

"It's you all over!"

So exclaims Tin Woodsman on rushing to Scarecrow's aid. In the real story (the movie version at least), Tin Woodsman behaves with great compassion and concern. Unlike Lion's observation that a trauma has occurred, Tin Woodsman's eye sees the result in the scattered effects: straw here, there, and everywhere. This is a significant next step. It, too, requires some examination at the biological level, which we will do now. In the next chapter, we will see most clearly where this is all leading when we examine the very visible changes in a person's life.

Trauma, in producing biological changes, results in altered thoughts, feelings, and behaviors. Part of this changing—the alteration in how nerve cells interrelate—we examined last chapter. Another part—the interrelationships of different communication systems in the body—we just discussed above. But one aspect of these phenomena we did not consider. Nerve cells convey their signals to one another through chemical messengers. Glands also use chemical messengers to convey instructions to different body organs. Changes in the functioning of these chemical messenger systems results in changes in thinking, feeling, and behaving because the messages being conveyed are being altered. Just imagine how we would act if we suddenly heard a loved one had died when what the person actually said was a loved one had *arrived*. The message we receive, whether accurate or not, dictates our body response. Trauma alters our internal communication systems and not only sends a terrible message itself but makes it harder than ever for us to later get other messages straight. Thus the very real effects seen by others and detected in the traumatized self are the result of changes that involve billions of chemical messengers working their magic at a microscopic level. These changes alter our message system and our way of reading scripts so that we act in ways that are often unproductive and unhealthy.

The whole situation is as if Scarecrow's normal functioning depended on exactly how each straw was stuffed into him and on how the straws communicated to one another. The trauma of the monkey experience literally knocked the stuffing out of him, rearranging the straw and changing the communication matrix he was accustomed to experiencing. The changing of the relationships among the various pieces of straw is a learning experience, but one with manifestly hurtful consequences. Fortunately for Scarecrow, his insides are only straw. For those of us with other ingredients the picture is not so simple.

There are a number of kinds of chemical messengers we depend upon. Some are very similar to one another, while others seem quite different from each other. Some are used to produce very specific or localized effects in the body, while others are more widespread in their use and consequences. Their specific effects in conveying information can be quite different, too. These different chemicals have very complex relationships to each other. Different nerve cell systems and glands rely on particular chemical messengers and not on others. Some chemical messengers depend on other chemicals to switch them on or off. Some are the products of changes in other messengers. Some vary in number and activity in proportion to the number and activity of other messengers. All in all, the body's use of these chemical messengers is complex, subtle, and delicately balanced.

Chemical messengers are involved in probably any human activity one can imagine. Some are needed to initiate sleep and some influence dreaming. If trauma affects the systems producing and using these chemical messengers, then sleep and dreaming will be affected. Some chemical messengers regulate our moods. If we have either an excessive functioning of some chemicals or a lack of functioning of others, we may experience dramatic changes in our feeling states. For example, one chemical messenger with widespread distribution and effects, is called serotonin (technically, its name is 5-hydroxytryptamine, but we'll stick to the nickname). The serotonergic system (i.e., the distribution system of this chemical messenger in the body) has a role in many important human activities, including sleep and the control of states of consciousness, and the regulation of sexual and reproductive processes, food intake, and mood. Generally speaking, we can say that high serotonergic function is good and low function is bad.

Sexual abuse trauma displays evidence of severely disrupting serotonergic function. The body, when examined and tested, frequently shows significantly lowered serotonergic function. The results can be dramatic. Mood disturbance can be displayed in depression. The person may become more aggressive and in some cases even direct that aggression toward others by continuing an abusive cycle. Or she or he may aggressively inflict the body by self-mutilation or even suicide. The messed up serotonergic system may contribute to altered states of consciousness. It may play a role in leading a person to substance abuse. Sexual functioning may become troubled. A person's regulation of food intake may be distorted, accompanied by disturbances in body image. Sleep may be severely disrupted, further aggravating other problems. In short, this one system being negatively impacted by abuse may contribute to many problems. By virtue of its interconnections with other chemical messenger systems, which it modulates, serotonin also contributes to a spreading pattern of messenger system dysfunctions.

All we have done here is describe briefly *one* chemical messenger system. But remember the reality is that 'everything is connected to everything else' in the body. From these tiny, tiny chemical messengers to the larger nerve cells in their manifold connections, to yet larger muscles and organs, to the symphony of parts that make a whole body, is a journey from a single snowflake to an avalanche that crashes through the mountain trees. We see the avalanche, and its grand horror may so arrest us that we fail to envision the snowflake that trembling set the entire mass in motion.

It does not look pretty on paper but the reality in the flesh is much more painful and confusing.

When the body's emergency systems are engaged because of trauma, some chemical messengers are pressed into heavy duty. This is quite adaptive in the short run because it helps us survive. But the body isn't built to operate like this for very long or very often. If we ask too much of these systems we are like a sprinter trying to run a marathon in the same way a hundred meter dash is run. The harmful consequences of overtaxing these systems require some separate consideration.

A bit ago I talked of messenger systems relaying information and commands so that the body reacted to the threat of a ball whizzing at the head. In that example, the moment comes . . . and then is gone. Either the person ducks in time, or gets clobbered. But what happens if this is not an unusual occurrence? What happens if a ball suddenly, unexpectedly being thrown at the head is something that happens just often enough to make it likely it will happen again?

If the body has to maintain a readiness for action, then some definite consequences will ensue. The person will soon develop a constant wariness, a hair-trigger response to sudden movements, and irritability from having to constantly be on guard. The peripheral nervous system component called the autonomic nervous system (ANS) will, through its sympathetic division, have to work overtime keeping the body ready. But that means some parts of the body will be getting extra supplies on a regular basis, whether they need them or not, while other parts will be left without the time and resources they need. For example, sympathetic arousal means digestive processes are blunted so that other systems can be at the ready. But that won't go on long before the digestive system—and the rest of the body, which depends on its role—begins to pay a stiff price. The chemicals the sympathetic system uses to keep things mobilized will become depleted, but because the system is still on, the body will try to change to accommodate the dwindling supply. It becomes a vicious cycle in which all the body's parts lose, and the whole person feels 'strung out' (as if all the body parts have been pulled apart), or 'burned out' (as if all the resources have been depleted leaving just a burn scar).

As stress researchers know, a stressor may last only a few hours, but its effects may last for years. This is often the case with trauma. When a condition of chronic stress response comes about because of a trauma that has occurred, and then persists even after the trauma has ceased and is unlikely to reoccur, then we have a condition called *post-traumatic stress*. In fact, it is often referred to as PTSD, with the letters representing post-traumatic stress *disorder*. The last word is significant. It means that the body is out of order, not working adaptively, and hence causing problems for the person. When the person responds to life after trauma as though the trauma were still present or ready to happen the next moment, then life is apt to be rather miserable.

Imagine Scarecrow, after being torn apart by the monkeys and reassembled by his friends, then obsessed with the memory of that event and the anxiety of its happening again. Certainly this would not be an entirely groundless concern. After all, the world has proved a very unfriendly place and he remains within the wicked witch's kingdom. On the other hand, he has a support system, he has been put back together, and the monkeys are clearly gone. There are no concrete indications they will return and no threat that they might. In such a circumstance, if he continually scans the skies to the degree he trips over the tree roots beneath his feet, is he acting adaptively? If he jumps and shudders at Lion's voice, is he responding prudently or over-reacting?

If Scarecrow experiences PTSD he may suffer from any number of symptoms that interfere with successfully managing his environment. He might become wary of others and distance himself from them even though they have given no evidence of being a threat. He may associate the attack with trees of a certain kind because he was assaulted in a forest and so choose to avoid the woods. He might find it difficult to sleep and be overwhelmed at times by sudden flooding memories of the trauma. He might grow increasingly edgy, irritable, or depressed. Doesn't sound like much fun, does it?

Remember, none of these things are willingly, consciously selected because they sound like a good idea. They are not fictitious responses but biological ones. While Scarecrow may avoid PTSD because he is, after all, merely made of straw, human beings are not made of such stern stuff. We are a boiling cauldron of chemicals and any one who messes with them is liable to mess the soup.

Putting Two and Two Together

I think it is hard for many of us to become comfortable with the idea that we are made of chemicals and that our thoughts, feelings, and behaviors rest on a chemical basis. But once we can accept that, then we can acknowledge that events that change the chemical mix change *us*. If our body's messenger system relies on chemicals to communicate, then think what incomplete, scrambled, garbled, or incorrect messages can result from radical changes in these systems. Human beings depend on living chemicals to grow and adapt; wound these chemicals and the basis for growth and life itself is seriously undermined.

Now if we add what we learned last chapter about the biology of learning to what we are discovering this chapter concerning how our bodies respond to the lessons, we end up with an interesting sum. The changes in how our nerve cells relate in modules can change the whole system in enduring ways so that the stress response meant to be an emergency response becomes instead a way of life. This is exactly what seems to have happened in the lives of many sexual abuse survivors.

The Scarecrow's Perspective

"Don't stand there talking—put me together! We've got to go find Dorothy!"

Finally, we come to Scarecrow's own response to his trauma, which is no less cognizant of his body than that of his friends. While not at all denying the reality of his companions' assessments—after all, he knows he needs to be put together—his comments are clearly focused and goal-directed. It has never surprised me that Dorothy can say to him just before leaving Oz that he is the one she feels closest to. Scarecrow, like Dorothy, is always active on his own behalf. *Rather than sitting in the tragedy, the successful response to trauma is to get help putting one's self back together and then getting on with the business of life at hand.* In Scarecrow's case, this business is helping someone else. But unlike many survivors of abuse who ignore their own needs in order to try to meet the needs of others, Scarecrow recognizes he must first be healed before he can help anyone else. He has his steps in proper order.

Would that all of us had the wisdom of the man of straw!

Chapter 5

OF BOUNDARIES & BORDERS

Between Kansas & Oz
Where do I belong? I feel as though I stand
with one foot in Kansas, the other in Oz.

I just want to go home!
But is Oz, or Kansas, my land?

Where do I belong? What pressing cause
tears at me, blurring my

boundaries along the borders
of Kansas and of Oz?

Where do I belong? Where is home?
I thought over the rainbow,

marching with a brave band. . . .
But I am so alone

twisted in Kansas, hunted in Oz.
Where do I belong? Who am I?

Crossing Borders

Dorothy's road is not an easy one. There is trauma in Kansas and Oz alike. In Kansas, a twister rips her from hearth and home. Her dream of being somewhere over the rainbow is not answered by a blue bird's happy trill but by the deafening roar of the cyclone and the vision of a wicked witch flying by her open window. Then, abruptly, she is in Oz. Almost at once this brilliantly colored land proves it, too, is a dangerous place. She is threatened by the wicked witch of the west. Her hopes pinned on rescue by a wonderful wizard, she instead is set by him on a dangerous quest. Midway through that quest she is snatched again from those she loves and deposited once more in a strange, unknown place. This time it is the wicked witch's fortress castle. In some perverse way it seems that no matter how much things change, they remain the same. Dorothy's life is filled with loss and danger.

Many of us can relate. The border between Kansas and Oz is one Dorothy is tossed across with violence. She may have dreamed of somewhere over the rainbow, but she did not ask to be forcibly thrown there. We who have survived trauma know what such border crossings are like. One moment our world is innocent, then violence rips away that innocence. We find ourselves, like Dorothy, knowing we are not in Kansas anymore.

But it is not merely the landscape that has changed. We have not just crossed a border from innocence to loss. *We* have been changed too. Our own boundaries have been altered, twisted by violation. Like Dorothy, we have found ourselves in a new, strange land. We are not in Kansas anymore. Like Scarecrow, our insides are scattered. There are bits of us over here and pieces of us over there. Like Tin Man, our hearts are broken. Like Cowardly Lion, our roar has been silenced.

And yet . . . Oz is not a land without hope. We are not alone. Others have gone before us. There are new companions to be found. The challenges of Oz are not insurmountable. The comforting gray hues of Kansas have been shattered by the dazzling colors of the rainbow. We have an unwanted, unwelcome, unwarranted new chance at life. We can either focus on the fact this chance is unwanted, unwelcome, and unwarranted, or we can grab it like Dorothy and her friends do and make the most of it, slaying evil witches along the way.

But first we have to be clear about where we are. Before Dorothy can succeed in Oz, she first has to know she has crossed the border from Kansas. This is a new land, with new rules. She must adapt. In some important ways, she is different too. Dorothy must recognize the changes within her as well as those outside her in the world. As she notes the border crossing, so she must reckon with the changes in her own boundaries.

Boundaries

Of course, there are boundaries . . . and then there are boundaries. Obviously, in Oz as in Kansas there are many kinds of boundaries. But all borders and boundaries are metaphors! Of course there are real physical features, such as rivers or mountain ranges that serve as borders between lands, yet what determines that one river is a border and another is just a river? A river becomes a border when we treat it *as if* it were a limit more distinct and formidable than it is by nature. Remember, the essence of a metaphor is that one thing is compared to another by treating it as though it were that other. We *make* borders and boundaries, and each is a metaphorical reality grounded in a physical one.

We can talk about physical borders, as we have been, which mark off one place from another. Consider the borders Dorothy crosses. Kansas and Oz are actually separated by two borders: the violence that pitches Dorothy into Oz in the first place, and the gentle clicking of her heels that transports her to her Kansan bed. These borders are not as obvious as rivers or mountains, but they are just as physical. Yet those borders, as important as they are, matter most to Dorothy and to us in how they affect more personal borders, what we call our 'boundaries.'

Picture these as somewhat flexible and permeable bubbles surrounding us. My bubble has a shape others can see as *me*. Boundary bubbles are transparent enough for us to see out and others to see in, but not so transparent that we can't keep things hidden inside. Everything that goes out from us, or comes in to us, must pass across the boundary. Ideally, our boundaries—our bubbles—are self-determined.

In working with survivors of sexual abuse it is very important to spend time considering personal boundaries because the normal sense of self-determination has been challenged. Instead of me deciding my own boundaries, someone else has forced entry across the borders of self and staked a claim to what I thought was mine. My bubble has been merged with this other person's, not by choice, but through the violence that is inherent in a lack of choice. To understand what happens to my bubble requires understanding the nature of boundaries.

A boundary, like a border between lands, marks *limits*. In the most fundamental sense, our boundaries are the limits of self. *This* is me; *that* is not me. *Here* I am; *there* I am not. Boundaries serve both to distinguish what is within us from what is outside us, and to preserve what is inside by mediating the forces without that seek entrance within. Without boundaries we would have no sense of who we are. When our boundaries are violated, we find our very self in question. Like Scarecrow, we leak our insides out into the world—and it isn't a pretty sight.

We are all like Dorothy too. She never fully leaves Kansas behind even while she is in Oz. We never completely leave the person we were before the abuse trauma; that is why we can talk appropriately about 'recovery.' Kansas remains the object of Dorothy's affection and desire. We, too, long for what we once had, before innocence was lost. Dorothy's own personal boundaries were first shaped there. It was in Kansas that the tornado struck. Our boundaries were shaped, to whatever degree, by our experiences before the trauma. Then the abuse violated those boundaries and twisted us up and around and deposited us in a new land. But just as Oz offers new opportunities for Dorothy where her boundaries can be reassessed and reformed, so too our worlds offer hope if we can find the brains, the heart, and the courage to pursue it.

But what do boundaries do for us in the limits that they set? Boundaries actually perform many functions, as I detail in another book, *Serving Human Experience: The Boundary Metaphor*. It is enough for now to note two: identity and mediation. The first key function of our boundaries is defining identity; boundaries form recognizable shapes so that we recognize a particular shape as being this person or thing and not another. Identity follows form, meaning we depend on specific characteristics visible in shape or action, and known reliably across time and circumstance. Ideally, the boundaries that form my bubble are distinctively mine.

The second key function of boundaries is *mediation*. Boundaries serve as portals for our interactions with the world. These bubbles preserve the integrity of identity by letting in what promotes growth and keeping out what constricts, hinders, or damages growth. In protecting us from harmful stimuli our boundaries are a primary defense system. When something forces its way in despite our boundary resistance, it is a violation. When these violations result in wounds, they are traumatic. Sexual abuse is a vicious, violent violation that wounds our boundaries.

With these two key functions in mind, let's return to Oz for a closer look.

Conversation Overheard on a Road in Oz

"Toto, how strange these borders are in Oz.
From Munchkin land to the Emerald City,
I can't keep the changes straight
in my head."
"Never fear," Scarecrow smiled, "because
along the yellow brick road one itty-bitty
step can take you from Oz's gate
right home to bed."
"That's right," Tin Woodsman chimed.
"Around here people just come and go
so fast your head will spin and swim
wondering where they've fled."
"And how will we find our way home at last
with a wicked witch out to do us in?
I wonder whether slow or fast
we can do as the Wizard said."
"Oh, bother," grumbled Lion. "You never mind,
Dorothy, *I'll* spit every foe
with these claws, and quickly trim
'em in bloody red!"
Dorothy beamed. "Others see straw and tin and kitty fur. Kansas' eyes find
brains in silly dancing flops,
a heart in rattling metal,
and steel in a Lion's purr.
"I've learned that if you walk in Oz you'll find
boundaries merely wait to let you grow
on past the senseless fearful stops
that thwart a person's mettle
to wisdom, love and courage."

Consider Dorothy's friends, as she does in the above poem. Each is very different from the others. They each have a recognizable shape by which they are known to others. But is the matter so simple as that? In fact, boundaries are like rainbow hues; staring at one color never resolves the wonder of the spectrum. Is the rainbow merely a single color? For that matter, is the rainbow only color? The joy of a rainbow is in presenting itself fresh and captivatingly different to every person—even while everyone agrees in calling it a rainbow. So, too, Dorothy recognizes that others may see "straw, and tin and kitty fur." But she sees "brains in silly dancing flops, a heart in rattling metal, and steel in a Lion's purr."

What Dorothy may be talking about is a facet of boundaries we can call *permeability*. It is easy enough to see how this relates to the function of mediation. Boundaries harden or soften to either keep out or let in various things from the outside world. A young child's clenched jaw against an unwanted food is a formidable barrier, but see how wide it grows when a pleasing delight is offered it! At a cellular level this permeability might be called the very glue of life, since it is by this mechanism that cells accept food, ward off invaders, and change their character so as to communicate with each other. Yet this permeability is important to identity, too. Through it a person's form takes on one appearance—soft and yielding, accepting and inviting—to one person and another appearance—hard and resistant, rejecting and distancing—to someone else. Permeability can reflect the less apparent aspects of form, such as vulnerability, warmth, openness, and flexibility. Thus, while others see just the surface shape that anyone can view from a distance, Dorothy sees the unique character shining in the forms from her closeness to them.

Boundaries also serve people as navigational buoys. They not only mark out where we leave off and others begin, they act as signals to direct the traffic of discourse between persons. As suggested in the poem, Dorothy's musings about the literal borders of Oz gives way to an insight about the metaphorical boundaries of her own person. Through dialog with her companions she realizes that boundaries only hold us in until such time as we are able to stretch them from the inside out toward personal growth. Leaving Oz is an extension of her own growing.

It is true that personal boundaries, by preventing harmful stimuli, may exist as a safety net against too rude a fall from experience, but their purpose is grander than just that defensive function. They simultaneously act as membranes instinctively flexing their way toward the light, warmth, and other ingredients of growth. It is this willingness to be flexible, to stretch our limits, that keeps us all at risk. If boundaries can be said to wait in any sense, Dorothy thinks they wait only for us to overcome our own inner obstacles, the "senseless fearful stops that thwart a person's mettle." But even so their waiting has a purpose, the moving past the obstacles to growth that we encounter and onward "to wisdom, love and courage."

Boundaries indicate limits, which in living, healthy systems are always seeking to expand. A boundary exists where Self and Other meet. A boundary divides inside from outside. A boundary both joins safety to growth and distinguishes one from the other. In every instance, a boundary is an *identifying* marker apart from which it is difficult, if not impossible, to discern the specific qualities or characteristics of a thing or person. But where boundaries identify living organisms, these borders are in constant flux because of the very nature of life. A net movement toward expansion occurs when the organism is healthy and a net movement toward constriction when the organism is wounded.

What we have said thus far we might in all fairness term 'the biology of body boundaries.' When forced to give a name to my position I like the term *biodynamic* because I insist we see living as growing. Life is *bio*—biological—and *dynamic*—energetic. But neither part—the biology nor the energy—is without form and void. The creation of life is order imposed on disorder; the destruction of life is disintegration into disorder. Apart from the forming and dissolving of boundaries we would be hard pressed to discern life from death. Biodynamics must necessarily be very concerned with boundaries. So when I consider sexual abuse, which violates boundaries, I see it through metaphors of wounding and dying, of disorder and loss of energy.

Wounded Boundaries

Sexual abuse is a disavowal of life. Instead of rewarding our natural instinct to expand, abuse encourages our boundaries to shrivel and become static. Or, where we succeed in not retreating to defend ourselves, we may be left with gaping holes that let too much of others in and too much of ourselves out. Then our expanding boundaries become too loose and diffuse. Our sense of self is left vague, overly accommodating, susceptible to easy wounding. So it would seem that abuse confronts us with awful choices: constrict, curl up, and defend what is left to us; try to remain where we are, frozen in place, neither living nor dying; or try to expand without regard to the gaping holes. In any case, we are changed—and not for the better.

Boundary violation is *never* a friendly act. Bluntly put, that's what enemies do. Abusers love to hide behind excuses about why a boundary could be crossed: 'her dress was an open invitation'; 'he is too young to know whether this is right or wrong'; 'this person is little more than a vegetable anyway, so where's the harm?' To any and all such lies I can only reiterate what I wrote years ago: "The provocatively clad young woman neither invites nor deserves to be raped. The innocent sexuality of a child neither invites nor deserves exploitation. The powerlessness or lack of understanding of a hospitalized person of diminished capacity neither justifies nor warrants sexual aggression. The point is unequivocal: no one deserves abuse."

In a moment we will draw six pictures, or models, for what may happen when our boundaries are violated. But first we must stand back and try to see a larger picture. The wounds of abuse leave boundaries that are torn and ragged. The functions of identity and mediation are both changed. In terms of identity, our very sense of self may be not only shaken, but altered such that we seem to become a stranger to our own self. In other words, the felt unity of body and soul is severed and our sense of self is thrown into question: Who am I *now*?

Our mediating function is also compromised. The normal rules for deciding what comes and goes across our borders have been forcibly changed by a greater power than our own. The old channels are forced along new courses. Our boundaries must adjust somehow. The ways in which they change dictate the new lines of communication we have with the world.

Six Models of Change

Sexual abuse trauma cannot help but change us. That does not mean it ends our lives. A trauma is a wound that *may* prove fatal, but is not necessarily deadly. We shall almost certainly bear some scars, but we must remember that scars show wounds that have healed. Let us take our gains where we can. The following six models indicate ways I have found are fairly common among survivors for personal boundaries to respond to sexual abuse trauma. These are initial responses that may prove enduring. However, as long as we live we have the chance to repair and redefine our personal boundaries.

Contraction

One way we might respond to abuse is through *contraction*. Our boundaries retreat. We may, for example, assume the shape of the identity we held when we last felt confident. So, if raped in adulthood we might retreat to adolescence. If violated as a teenager we might become more childlike—or childish. This is a defensive reaction to the trauma. If we cannot move forward safely, perhaps we can find safety in retreat. Our bubble shrinks back upon itself, conserving its energy. We may feel stronger as a result, but others are likely to see us in the retreat we are really pursuing.

Closing

A second way our boundaries may react is by *closing* down, stopping all traffic across them, and coming to a complete stop. The shock of abuse brings about a kind of freezing. Our identity is stuck, our mediating overwhelmed. This radical solution has to be temporary because we cannot survive without some transactions. But this radical stoppage buys time to catch the breath. Afterwards, the boundaries must transition into one of the other models of response.

Collapse

A third way our boundaries might respond to abuse is through catastrophic *collapse*. This is perhaps the most terrifying of all responses. The sense of self flees and the world comes crashing in. Nothing from outside can be stopped. The other defines the self. Yet, as terrible as this is, collapse does more than reduce us to empty ruins. It clears ground for new construction. At some point we must resume living, and that means rebuilding our boundaries, reforming our bubble, resuming our efforts at growth. Precisely because this response is so catastrophic, if we survive it, then we may actually be more quickly on the mend than others whose response is less radical.

Compensation

A fourth way we might respond is through *compensation*. As the bubble of our boundaries feels force against it, the bubble compensates by extending out somewhere else. An indentation at one point is matched by a bulge, or bulges, elsewhere. Thus, overdeveloping our cognitive abilities may compensate for a lack of feeling brought about by the wounds we have received. We may feel wounded in trust and compensate by becoming a caregiver. The ways in which we might compensate for the penetrating wounds of abuse are innumerable and individual. The energy displaced from one part of the bubble is fed to another region.

Containment

A fifth way abuse might be responded to by our boundaries is by *containment*. I sometimes refer to this as the 'balloon model,' because like a balloon being filled with more and more air, we continue to stretch our boundaries, trying to encompass both self and other. Like the balloon's surface, the boundary bubble stretches evenly in all directions. Energy is redistributed without awkward bulging in one or another spot. Increased pressure, though, brings the boundary nearer and nearer to the point beyond which it cannot stretch. A little more energy and suddenly it bursts. What is inside explodes outward, leaving profound emptiness behind and sudden, unexpected, shocking damage all around.

Concealment

A sixth way our boundaries might respond to trauma is through *concealment*. I sometimes refer to this as the 'post-partum model,' because like a woman who has just given birth, her shape may return to similar to what it was before but still show stretch marks. What has happened is that the abuse pressure has been spread across the boundary bubble, forcing it inward, but when that pressure leaves, the bubble bounces back. All appears to be as it was before. There are no visible signs of damage. Only by close inspection can the tell-tale stretch marks of the trauma be found. The presence of these marks both testify to what has happened and indicate a new susceptibility that needs recognition and care.

Please know that these six ways of response do *not* tell the entire story. The ways our boundaries adapt to abuse trauma are *transitional*. Remember, life is always about the instinct to grow. As long as we choose to live, we give ourselves opportunities to change our boundaries. This little book is about using helpful metaphors to provide imaginative experiences to counterbalance the harmful ones we have experienced. Through accompanying Dorothy and her friends in Oz we can develop stronger, healthier boundaries along our own road here in Kansas.

All along we have been keeping one foot in Oz and another in Kansas as we reflect on sexual abuse. Last chapter we considered three perspectives on trauma. The focus remained on the body even though Tin Woodsman, Lion, and Scarecrow each had a different point of view. We examined the nature of changes in the body that accompany trauma and how these underlie the effects we may see in people who have survived sexual abuse. However, we did not detail the often very visible and disturbing effects we may notice as a result of abuse. These can, and often do affect the way we feel, think, and behave. Our memory may be affected. So might be our mood. Our previous life goals may seem unrealistic and be given up. Our motivation may falter.

All of these kinds of effects may be related to the changes to our boundaries that result from trauma. I hope by now we are all clear that we *are* our bodies, whether they be made of flesh, or straw, or tin, or kitty fur. There is no 'self' apart from the biology that makes us. Our body boundaries set limits to all our personal boundaries. As we have seen in previous chapters, we can picture ourselves as a soup of boiling chemicals. But that picture may not be a tasty one! We may prefer to imagine the body as a community of life. The self is a living collective of distinct but not separate living pieces that unite, without senseless fusing, into an intelligent, purposeful whole. That whole is a song played and sung by the body.

Within us, each living piece has its own shape, place, and goals. Each moves in concert with all the other pieces. When one voice is stilled, another takes its place. Always the song of the whole, the grand opera of life, is sung. The borders of the players interlock like musical notes splayed across the score before the conductor's eyes. But unlike notes frozen on a page, music swells with life, growing now quieter, and now more forceful with the quickening tempo of change.

Trauma is a discordant note that changes the sound of the whole composition. Like a brass player failing to hit a high note at the crescendo of the concert, abuse focuses our attention on one note at the expense of all the other instruments. It is too insistent an intrusion to ignore. We cannot help but hear it, even if we bend all our might to ignore it. It has changed the music and sooner or later the reality of the new musical score must be addressed. But though the note of trauma rings harshly in our ears, it remains just one part of the whole. As long as we live we have the conductor's power to alter the score and rebalance the orchestra.

Every piece in an orchestra has to know its part. It is up to the conductor to determine the role of each instrument, its prominence and its limits. We must do the same with our lives. Our personal boundaries exist to protect and define us. Awareness of our boundaries is an important first step to making them more effective both for defense and self-expression. In fact, I can go even further by saying that we *must* attend to our boundaries because they are essential to who we are and to becoming who we want to be.

We human beings have all kinds of boundaries, from the physical borders of our skin and other sense organs to complicated psychosocial ones. Sexual abuse penetrates many layers, from the fleshly surface to the deepest, most hidden self-concept. There is a chain here: a physical violation of our boundaries affects us psychologically, which affects us physically. Well-informed mental health professionals understand that it is rarely the initial physical act of sexual abuse that does all the harm. Instead, it is the *context* of relationships, feelings, and meanings that make the momentary physical acts so psychologically enduring. We may add that violations of psychosocial boundaries inevitably result in biological alterations, such as we have already considered. These provide the ultimate links in the chain that binds us to our abuser—a continuing insult felt in our bodies. In sum, what starts as a physical act by someone else is transformed within our bodies' boundaries into lingering physical effects, both those we experience as bodily and those that plague the mind. It is to those effects of these boundary violations we must now turn.

Chapter 6

STRAW & TIN & KITTY FUR

Different

"I am different somehow," Dorothy told her friend.
Scarecrow put a finger to his head. "How?"
"I don't know," Dorothy answered with a frown.

"Well, I remember when I was on the mend,"
her companion mused. "And now
I'm different, too."

"Of course," said Dorothy with a smile.
"Once you were strewn all about,
and then you pulled yourself together."

"Well, you've had your share of trial
and trouble, too," said Scarecrow. "Perhaps your route,
like mine, has changed you forever."

Dorothyitis

Dorothy cannot survive a tornado and not be changed. We cannot experience sexual abuse and not be altered. As soon as Dorothy confesses to Toto that she doesn't think they are in Kansas anymore, she reveals her awareness of change. The storm has transported her; Oz will transform her. We, too, have been carried by our experiences into a new land. We bear the marks of it. This chapter details some of the changes we may have experienced.

But first, let's linger a moment with Dorothy in Oz. Looked at from the standpoint of the citizens of Oz, it is Dorothy who is odd. In fact, for the wicked witches of the land, Dorothy is a fatal affliction. They die of 'Dorothyitis!' Nor are they alone infected. Her companions are each profoundly affected.

They, too, have caught Dorothyitis. She is a strange experience who turns their world upside-down. To get on with their lives in a post-Dorothy Oz they must first be honest about what Dorothyitis has done to them.

All profound experiences, from the glory of love to the bitter lie of sexual abuse, change us. To manage the effects of that change requires us to do what Scarecrow, Tin Woodsman, and Lion do: reckon honestly what has happened. To their immense credit, all three friends prove willing and capable of doing this assessment. Each achieves insight into what Dorothyitis has meant for them and as a result their learning is profound. In a post-Dorothy Oz they can live richly meaningful lives.

So can we. It certainly is more fun to detail the glad changes wrought by an experience like love, but it is necessary to confront the changes brought about by abuse. Otherwise, our ignorance will continue to wound us. We cannot learn all we can learn from the experience unless we look at it closely. To bind up a wound for proper and full healing means assessing the changes and counting the damage.

So what is the visible damage from the cyclone of sexual abuse? Have you ever seen the after-effects of a tornado? Every scene is different, even though they all look alike. There is chaos and debris everywhere, but the specific stuff strewn around varies from place to place. So it is with sexual abuse: it all looks the same; it all looks different.

Mental health professionals pretty much agree that anyone exposed to situations of extreme stress, or trauma, are likely to suffer a variety of consequences, some of them short-lived, and others long-term. The most significant of these might include changes in the person's basic sense of self, their unique character, or what others see as their personality. Given what we have considered in the last few chapters this should come as no surprise. So we ought to be able to recognize sexual abuse survivors cannot be stereotyped as to how they will be affected; every person's change is unique. Simply put, there is no pattern of 'symptoms' (after-effects) that can allow someone with confidence to say, "*That's* what sexual abuse looks like!" It looks like what it looks like—as individual as the person affected.

If the effects are unique in how each of us experience them, then there is no one answer for all of us. Looking at the effect of sexual abuse in our lives is a highly individual matter. Like it or not, we are alone in the uniqueness of our own experience and its pain. That does not mean, however, that there aren't some consequences that seem more common than others, and we may find we share some effects with fellow survivors, each in our own way. As awful as it is to realize others have had to endure cyclones like the one we survived, there is power and hope knowing we are in the company of *survivors* who, like Dorothy, found the brains, the heart, and the courage to sustain them along their own yellow brick roads. If they can do it, so can we!

And there is this consolation: no matter how unique Scarecrow, Tin Woodsman, and Cowardly Lion may all be, they share a constellation of 'symptoms' by virtue of each of them having been infected by 'Dorothyitis.' All three are fiercely loyal to a little Kansas girl. All three experience growth and liberation through their experiences *of* her as well as *with* her. All three are united in common goals: getting to the Emerald City to see the wizard, bringing back the wicked witch's broom, helping Dorothy. In short, no matter their individual dissimilarities, they share a set of recognizable features centered around Dorothy. If we regarded their experience as pathological and connected it to Dorothy, we could claim that she was the disease with which they were infected and the things just mentioned constitute their symptoms.

So Who's Got What?

But what if we have symptoms and can't remember catching the disease? Scarecrow, Tin Woodsman, and Lion are lucky in that they all are quite clear about their experience of Dorothy. Similarly, as unpleasant as it was, Dorothy remembers the cyclone and the wicked witches. For those whose experience of trauma remains clear to their mind's eye, linking symptoms and cause seems much easier. But what about the rest of us?

Many of us who survive sexual abuse trauma have little or no recollection of it, at least for a while. We may, in fact, be quite resistant to the suggestion that our experiences include one like abuse. The effects of sexual abuse trauma commonly do not present themselves in a nice, neat, tidy clinical picture that makes identifying the trauma an easy task. Therefore, many experts in the area of sexual abuse resist the notion of developing any formal kind of diagnostic criteria to try to determine abuse as a causal factor where it is not remembered, or where it is denied but the clinician suspects otherwise.

Yet, in practice, no clinician can avoid forming some framework to try to resolve situations where a person wonders if sexual abuse occurred, or wants to remember a childhood shrouded in gaps and fragmented memories, or vigorously disputes the suggestion despite presenting a profile the therapist has seen before where abuse is known to have occurred. The sad fact is that often the only irrefutable 'proof' that abuse has happened may be the presence of a sexually transmitted disease in a young child. In other words, most of the time we have no definitive proof. All the evidence is circumstantial.

Reading the Stars

In Kansas every Professor Marvel relies on photo snapshots to see more clearly in the crystal ball. Yet we—survivors and therapists alike—crave some concrete guidelines, based on what has been observed in many, by many, in order to better manage the uncertainties. In sum, we feel a need to make responsible stabs at shaping a diagnostic constellation even if not all the glittering stars fit within it. In time, the signs of the zodiac will form subtypes that will help us navigate the universe and discriminate among the various things we find in this darkest of skies.

The only alternative I see to developing a constellation of sexual abuse trauma signs is to slide into the chaos of mere guesswork. I think that sexual abuse in general constitutes a constellation of recognizable features, while specific instances can and do vary in the number and kind of other associated symptoms. We don't need to be dogmatic in order to form and use a map. As long as it helps us accurately get where we need to, it won't matter if it is imperfect. The act of traveling with it as our guide will mean learning more to redraw the map as time goes on.

Any ship's captain learns to know where the ship is on the high seas by learning to read the stars. It is not, however, required that the captain have names for all of them. What is more important is recognizing the relationships some of them have to one another or to the earth. So it is with recognizing sexual abuse. I am not claiming that certain discrete symptoms are invariably present to make a diagnosis of sexual abuse possible. What I am claiming is that sexual abuse can be inferred from specific patterns of symptoms. Just as abuse trauma presents itself in subtypes of trauma constellations, of which sexual abuse is one, so sexual abuse often presents itself in specific patterns.

I will not attempt to delineate all, or even some of the patterns of symptoms by which sexual abuse can be inferred. That effort requires a book of its own. My more modest goal here is to identify major symptoms that are aspects of most, if not all, of the different patterns. Each of these major signs is a visible reflection of the biological alterations that have occurred in the body through the invasiveness of the trauma. Moreover, it seems reasonable to me to expect that eventually we shall be able to develop broad profiles of sexual abuse effect constellations based upon a better understanding of the underlying physiology of distinctive biological patterns.

As it is, often the uncovering of trauma in the past is the result of dysfunctions in the present. Remember, abuse is unnatural; it disrupts the natural order. The major signs of abuse trauma can group together to form a distinctive pattern recognizable as a psychological 'dis-order.' Unfortunately, survivors as a group tend to have patterns of problems that more often fit criteria for psychological diagnosis than do other folk. We have been left wounded and vulnerable, so why be surprised we show the wounds?

The effects of abuse may manifest as a medical or behavioral problem. Some research suggests that children and young people who have been abused are far more likely to manifest such problems than their peers. When we add it all up, our likelihood of showing disturbance in psychological functioning, body functioning, or behavior is much higher than for other people. We are, as they say, an 'at risk' group. So we are hardly alone when we face significant problems as a result of a significant negative experience. We are in the company of survivors. And the bottom line of that word 'survivor' means that despite all the nasty after-effects, we are *still here*.

More good news can be told. It isn't inevitable that trauma produce disorder of a degree strong enough to be clinically significant. Thankfully, some among us who experience sexual abuse trauma manage to survive without severe disturbances. We vary in resiliency; some of us experience less distress than others. Those of us who experience greater distress may be less resilient, but that does not make us weaker-minded or morally inferior. It merely means we are made in such a way and have had such life experiences that we are not as rapid at bouncing back from injury. So if we do have a disturbing level of disorder it is important to confront it and to seek help. There is nothing wrong or shameful in seeking assistance with problems we have not been able to overcome yet, or on our own. Dorothy shows brains, heart and courage both in being patient with her process of traveling and in accepting companions.

Human variability in biological makeup and environmental situations equals diversity in response to sexual abuse. We saw that last chapter with how our personal boundaries might respond to abuse trauma. Now we note the same is true of the visible effects we may experience. These differences are both of kind and degree, as Dorothy's friends in Oz show. Even though Scarecrow, Tin Woodsman, and Lion all experience Dorothyitis, they are not all affected by it to the same extent or in exactly the same way.

How Do You Navigate on a Cloudy Night?

However, they do share, to some degree, a pattern made up of certain similar symptoms and a generally recognizable course of progress. If the Wizard of Oz were a doctor, he would most certainly be interested in developing a model to understand better this phenomenon which, over time, seems to spread throughout his land, affecting Munchkins and monkeys alike. The various symptoms may not prove Dorothyitis, but they do indicate the possibility of its presence. The symptoms may at least prompt the wizard to wonder if this new agent called Dorothyitis, known to produce such symptoms, is at work. While he may not be able to rule out other causes, why should he ignore Dorothyitis as a possible one?

Earlier, I used the picture of a ship's captain navigating by the stars. As both a survivor and a helper, I am keenly conscious of the importance of reading the 'stars' related to abuse and navigating by them. Symptoms tell pieces of a larger story. But what if the night is a cloudy one? What if the symptoms suggest abuse but there has been no declaration of it? What then?

This is delicate ground. While a physician or therapist who detects symptoms of sexual abuse trauma should consider that important, how should they pursue the matter? If we have no conscious recollection of such an experience, and so have no idea of it, what then? Of course, the doctor or therapist has no certain knowledge of what we have experienced and cannot read minds, so does not even know whether we have knowledge we are holding back. Yet, if he or she ventures to ask about such an experience, might not the suggestion be enough to implant a false idea, produce false memories, and lead the course of treatment into a land of fantasy?

These are serious questions. I do not regard a professional's proper task as playing detective to prove or disprove whether a particular experience has occurred. To me the proper task is to render help based on what is visible right now. I have strong reservations about suggesting to anyone that they may have had a traumatic experience they do not recall. While I am convinced such things happen, I am equally convinced it is not my task or any helper's task to prove it. There is enough work to be done with the symptoms at hand.

I think good practice is preventive practice. When I interview someone for the first time, I include questions ranging over a number of areas. I ask about habits of life, about medical history, and about how life is going right now. I ask about the past, the present, and future hopes. I inquire about people. I also specifically ask if abuse has occurred.

Of course, there is no certainty that this person, still relatively a stranger to me, will answer truthfully if abuse has occurred or is ongoing. There is also the possibility it has happened in the past and been put out of the conscious mind. So if the person provides no confirmation of the experience, I do not pursue it in the interview. I do, however, note all symptoms.

If the symptoms suggest an abuse experience the person has either denied or claims no recall for, then I tread carefully indeed. Rather than risk implanting by suggestion an idea the person might seize upon to provide an answer to the puzzle of her or his condition—which can lead to creating false memories—I pursue a more cautious path. I stay open to possibilities and engage in *as if* thinking while I work. In other words, I remain watchful for plausible explanations for what I am seeing and, where it is helpful, act *as if* I know the answer. This is a creative fiction and I am careful to remind myself that I don't *know*—I only suspect. But I keep my suspicions to myself. I can help people even where the cause of their symptoms remains forever unknown.

If the person asks, "Is it possible I was abused?" I take a different course. I follow their lead if they want to explore the possibility. By staying behind them I minimize the risk of leading them astray. Every person has a right to know her or his own experience. And that is the real point: the experience is not mine, but the client's. I can only respect it by doing my best not to contaminate it. All the truth any of us need will emerge as it is most needed.

The Constellations

In the remainder of this chapter we shall focus on a number of the more prominent and likely effects following from sexual abuse trauma. Let me offer what I see as ten primary *sign heads* (i.e., signs that encompass a number of related symptoms) important in concluding that sexual abuse may be reasonably inferred. I do not claim that each of these is equal in importance, nor that any is unique to this kind of trauma. In fact, I explicitly claim only that the presence of one or more of these sign heads should alert us to the possibility of sexual abuse as a factor and that only in relying on the detection of one or another specific pattern of symptoms should an *as if* hypothesis of sexual abuse trauma be provisionally held.

Here are the ten primary sign heads:

➢ *Distressing awareness of change or difference.*
➢ *Body disturbance.*

> *Learning & memory dysfunctions.*
> *Enduring perception of threat.*
> *Hampered ability to trust.*
> *Lowered self-esteem.*
> *Grief.*
> *Reflective feeling complexes.*
> *Mood disorders.*
> *Difficulties with behavioral control.*

It is important to note that these signs may manifest in a variety of ways with significant differences among individuals. For each sign head a brief description can be offered. It also is useful to enumerate some of the more commonly reported symptoms. With these symptom lists we can consider each sign head more carefully.

Distressing Awareness of Change

We have spent some time noting the reality of biological change wrought by abuse trauma. Psychological changes reflect the underlying biological ones. A significant change is the awareness of change itself. This awareness may be cognitive, emotional, or behavioral. The awareness of change may take one or more of the following symptom forms:

> Altered awareness.
> Generalized sense of *dis*-ease.
> Sense of stigmatization.
> Dissociative episodes.
> Intrusive thought/feeling/memory episodes.
> Sleep changes.
> Relationship problems.

How does Dorothy know that she and Toto are in Oz? Well, of course it's obvious. For one thing, Oz is in color! But remember, Dorothy does not know at first that she is in Oz. She only seems reasonably certain she isn't in Kansas anymore. Isn't the case the same with sexual abuse? I think the first characteristic of sexual abuse trauma is that the person has an awareness at some level that something has changed for the worse. I know that seems hardly remarkable. The same might be said for any factor that brings a person to seek help. But with sexual abuse the specific indicators almost always include one or more of the symptoms listed above. Of these various symptoms special significance should be granted to *dissociative episodes*, which are primary signs of trauma. Other especially noteworthy signs are intrusive thought/feeling/memory episodes, which frequently signal the emergence trauma related issues, and relationship problems, particularly as these reflect issues of parenting, difficulties with trust, or sexual dysfunction.

Body Disturbance

How could the alterations of body biology not result in some level of body disturbance? If a bad pizza affects us in a body disturbance surely it is not too much to suggest that the trauma of sexual abuse will do the same! Because this trauma is a violation at such a fundamental level of being, the body systems affected are likely to be foundational ones like perception, digestion, sexuality, sleep, or somatic sensation. Here are some of the more commonly associated symptoms of body disturbance:

➢ Body image distortions.
➢ Distrust of one's own perceptions.
➢ Eating disorders (anorexia, bulimia).
➢ Medical problems (e.g., chronic pain, allergies, headaches).
➢ Gender identity confusion.
➢ Sexual dysfunctions.
➢ Sleep disturbances.

Personal identity begins early in life with our body awareness. Self-image is in significant measure *body* image. That does not mean just how we look. Our self-image as influenced by our body image includes how it feels to occupy *this* flesh, in all its glories and imperfections. It involves how we sense our world, move about in it, and take it in. When our bodies are disturbed, *we* are disturbed. No matter what else we may do to help ourselves, we cannot neglect this disturbance in the body. Until it is set right, our self is not right. So counseling that neglects the body only serves to reinforce a false sense that the mind exists apart from the body. We must forge a partnership with all our parts to feel whole—and to know our own unique place in the world. Dorothy can keep her bearings in Oz in large part because she and Toto retain body integrity.

Accordingly, any body disturbance merits thinking of trauma as a possible antecedent, and when the resulting effects are seen in an area like sexual dysfunction the possibility of sexual abuse should be seriously considered, especially if at least one additional sign under this head also appears.

Learning & Memory Dysfunctions

The alleged effects of abuse trauma on memory are the most controversial aspect of the entire field. However, as previous chapters have shown, all learning and memory is housed in the body and has a biological basis. To think that the changes produced by trauma might affect learning and memory is hardly an outrageous leap of logic. The following symptoms are those most often reported:

➢ Distorted memories (i.e., misremembering to minimize pain).
➢ Learning fixations.
➢ Partial amnesia.
➢ Repression of memories.

When Dorothy returns to Kansas and tries to tell her loved ones about Oz, she realizes that already the experience has taken on a dream-like quality. Did she really visit a magical land, or—as Auntie Em suggests—dream a silly thing? Memories are almost always a very important matter to survivors of trauma. They may have been perplexed for years by amnesia, fragments and images, or feelings and sensations that all point to something missing. Some folk regard this as the single most distinguishing hallmark of the presence of unresolved past trauma. It is important enough that the next chapter is principally concerned with it.

Enduring Perception of Threat

Some experiences in life are so profound that the lesson they present is indelibly learned. For example, we only have to touch a hot stove once to know we don't want to ever do *that* again! We are forever after more vigilant around hot stoves. Would that we could have as much success ensuring trauma never happens again! But because many of us are not in a position to ensure that by our own actions, we develop a hypervigilance toward threats that can be associated with more violations. Over time we may develop one or more of the following relatively stable emotional sets that represent an enduring perception of threat:

➤ Anxiety.
➤ Fear.
➤ Exaggerated startle response.
➤ Hypervigilance.
➤ Post-traumatic stress symptoms.

Remember how the Munchkins, witnesses to the demise of the wicked witch of the East when Dorothy's house landed on her, can scarcely believe the evidence of their own eyes? They must undertake an elaborate verification of her death. So great has been her tyranny over them that even incontrovertible evidence of her end can barely overcome the irrational fear of her. Extreme, especially prolonged, instances of trauma excite our bodies to a near permanent 'red alert' condition. Trauma experts commonly point to this persistent perception of threat as a characteristic of post-trauma adaptation. Even when we *know* the source of the threat is gone, we may *feel* endangered. We see the world through glasses colored by the less than rosy experience of abuse.

An ability to recognize the post-traumatic stress syndrome is important to the detection of unresolved sexual abuse trauma.

Hampered Ability to Trust

Trust is both receptive and outreaching. The violation of sexual abuse undermines trust. It lessens receptivity as we become more defensive to protect ourselves. Instead of reaching out with confidence, if we reach out at all that reaching may take on a more desperate quality. Those of us wounded by persons we depend on for safety are especially hurt because we have no choice but to keep on seeking safety from someone who keeps on endangering us. How could such a context not have a lasting effect? These may include:

> Attachment problems.
> Abandonment and/or engulfment fears.
> Dependency.
> Intimacy problems.
> Isolation.

Glinda, the good witch, is still a witch. In Dorothy's understanding upon arriving in Oz, a witch is by definition a being of malevolence. Dorothy stands incredulous at the suggestion that Glinda, a being of softness and light, can be called a witch. Perhaps it is in part because of Glinda's recognition of this confusion in Dorothy that she does not ask the girl from Kansas to trust the witch from Oz. Instead, Glinda sets Dorothy on the yellow brick road where, in the course of time, she meets companions who win her trust and help bring her to the moment when she can trust Glinda enough to invoke the magic inside herself. Sexual abuse survivors often have pronounced difficulties trusting others because those to whom they looked for safety and guidance betrayed that trust and misused their positions of authority. However, because issues of trust may reflect so many developmental traumas and problem issues, I do not think this one sign alone is ever enough to warrant suspicion of sexual abuse. Any symptom under this head must be accompanied by symptoms from other sign heads.

Lowered Self-esteem

Few topics have received more attention in the last generation or so than self-esteem. The concept is simple in essence: self-esteem is how we value ourselves. Certain experiences teach us that we are valued by others, which encourages us to value ourselves. Other experiences demean us and prompt internal questions about our worth. A very long list of symptoms reflecting lowered self-esteem could be created. However, the following are associated with the effects of sexual abuse trauma—though I must emphasize that these symptoms can result from any number of experiences.

> Apologetic to excess.
> Awkward sense of always being in the way.
> Devaluation of efforts and accomplishments.
> Inability to receive compliments, gifts.
> Labels used by self like 'loser,' 'a failure,' etc.
> Lack of assertiveness.
> Over solicitousness.
> Sense of being deficient, incompetent, etc.
> Value judgments by self as 'bad,' 'evil,' 'sinful,' etc.
> Victimization patterns.

It is easy to see how self-blame, which we considered in chapter 2, and self-image are related. But a look at the list above shows just how many ways low self-esteem may be displayed. Dorothy grows in self-esteem as she succeeds in her journey. Yet how can we forget her periodic bouts of anxious apologies and efforts at appeasement? Only with difficulty can she bring herself to be assertive. Still, Dorothy does grow in these respects—and so, too, can survivors of sexual abuse.

While it is easy to make too much of self-esteem, which once was seen almost like a panacea to cure all our bad feelings, we ought not belittle it. Self-esteem quite literally means the regard and respect we hold for ourselves. Survivors of abuse can, figuratively speaking, lose our voice because we no longer regard ourselves as having anything to say, or fear no one will listen because of who we have become. Like trust issues, low self-esteem is so pervasive a problem it cannot be used by itself as a probable indicator of sexual abuse. On the other hand, it is probably safe to say that sexual abuse does not happen without lowered self-esteem as a result.

Grief

For myself, I know no other word that springs more readily to mind about my life than the word *loss*. The sense of loss following trauma can be pronounced and enduring. But the grief spawned by the wounds we experience may take a number of forms. Here are some well-known ones:

➢ Bargaining.
➢ Detachment.
➢ Denial (including minimizing).
➢ Loss.
➢ Rage.
➢ Uncomplicated bereavement (grief depression).

We all know what loss is like. It is a universal human experience. When Dorothy journeys to the land beyond the rainbow she loses contact with Auntie Em and Uncle Henry. When she leaves Oz to return to Kansas, she loses the presence of Scarecrow, Tin Woodsman, and Lion. These losses bring tears to her eyes and to mine, because I care about Dorothy.

Sexual abuse means loss, too. Or more accurately, it means *losses*—for they are many. Perhaps the most often remarked upon loss, especially for those of us abused in childhood, is the loss of the innocence we associate with that stage of life. We expect that children should be able to explore and enjoy the wonders of sexual intimacy in their own time, at their own speed, with consenting peers. This loss inspired therapist Beverly Engel to entitle her book on sexual abuse *The Right to Innocence*. Every child has a natural right to grow up innocent of what sexual abuse forces upon him or her. In being abused, survivors have lost an important right, though what we later feel most heavily is not the sense of a *right* displaced, but the lost *innocence* itself.

The losses just seem to go on and on. They bring the flood of grief as we may mourn the loss of our confidence in the goodness of the world, the safety of others, and our ability to protect ourselves. We may lose all confidence in our ability to control our lives since we could not even control our own body. We may give up hope that we can attain or maintain a satisfying relationship with someone else, especially a satisfying sexual relationship. So many losses! Too many losses. And these losses are not always mourned consciously, yet they find ways to work themselves out as symptoms we need to recognize.

Reflective Feeling/Behavior Complexes

Some responses to trauma seem almost instinctive. They are what I would term *reflexive*—they happen without thought. Others are mediated to some degree. They are filtered through the complex psychosocial environments we inhabit. We react along lines reflecting how we sense we *should* respond. These kinds of feelings and behaviors rest upon a cognitive judgment formed by our total experience of life. The specific experience of trauma is filtered and interpreted by this judgment even though we may not be consciously aware we are making it. Some of the signs of that process might include:

➢ Blame, guilt & anger directed at self.
➢ Blame, guilt & anger directed at some other.
➢ Paranoia.
➢ Powerlessness, emptiness & hopelessness.

This sign head's title requires a note of explanation. I distinguish between two general groups of emotions: reflexive (essentially subcortical in origin) and reflective (mediated by cortical areas). A reflective feeling is secondary in character and should not be confused with a primary emotion. It might help to conceive of reflective feelings as those feelings we decide we *ought* to have. With practice and cultural help we can make these pretty automatic. In a shame-based cultural, for example, shame may be elicited by any number of 'oughts.' In Oz, the Cowardly Lion wants desperately to feel brave rather than afraid. As 'the king of the forest' it is the way he imagines he ought to feel. The important thing here is a consciousness that certain reflective feelings cluster (such as guilt or anger with blaming behavior). When a cluster is seen and the referent identified (e.g., the self or some particular other), some indication of abuse trauma may surface. This seems to me an area especially needing research attention.

Mood Disorders

When feelings linger, we may label them 'moods.' Certain moods are not only unpleasant, they hamper our development. Yet each of the feelings characteristic of the mood has a valuable purpose. Anxiety is an early detection alert system that helps prepare us for future events or situations. When it serves this purpose and then ends it is adaptive. When it persists regardless of what the future brings, then it hinders us and is unhealthy. Depression serves a natural conservation of energy that affords us a chance to regroup. As a temporary response to loss it is rational and beneficial. But when it persists or deepens so that we cannot function as we need to, then the depression is a serious condition. Feelings can become moods which can be become disordered conditions. Sexual abuse trauma is commonly associated with one or more of the following:

- ➤ Anxiety.
- ➤ Panic.
- ➤ Depression.

Dorothy's companion Lion is almost perpetually afflicted by anxiety. It is his identifying mood. Prominent moods among sexual abuse survivors are anxiety, panic, and depression. Yet these are commonly reported clinical conditions and may arise from any number of causal factors. Like certain other sign heads, this one is not in itself sufficient to suspect sexual abuse; it requires some other referent. But sexual abuse commonly means one or another such mood is a problem, often very persistently. There is hardly any other area that has been more written about than mood disorders and I believe most of us will profit from pursuing further reading in this regard.

Difficulties with Behavioral Control

Life goes on no matter what happens within it. No matter what we experience, we still have to generate behavior of some kind. But the distortion of our boundaries by the wounds of abuse typically generate difficulties with behavioral control. The disruption of the mechanisms by which we understand and regulate our behavior can get us into serious problems. Here are some of the difficulties survivors may struggle with over time:
- ➤ Addictions.
- ➤ Aggression resulting in harm to self or others.
- ➤ Eating problems (diet & weight control issues).
- ➤ Impulsive acts.
- ➤ Obsessive-compulsiveness (or perfectionism).
- ➤ Passivity.
- ➤ Promiscuity.

The list under this heading could be much expanded but the signs offered are all important ones. Special attention should be given to any aggression that is sexual in nature, regardless of who it may be directed against. In Oz, with very little provocation from Scarecrow, the apple trees impulsively throw away the very fruit they are zealously trying to protect. Impulsive behavior very often means we work against our own best interests and better judgment. Control is a major theme for most sexual abuse survivors and will be discussed further in chapter 9.

What's Your Sign(s)?

Although the above lists are not intended to be comprehensive, they are intended to be representative. I hope it is evident why I have resisted trying to specify distinctive sexual abuse patterns here. That work truly requires a book of its own, and a sizeable one at that. But by being honest about our own symptoms we can piece together a picture of the pattern of effects abuse trauma has drawn in our own lives.

Dorothy knows she is in Oz by the signs of *difference*. Sexual abuse is often discovered from this same ability to detect our differences from others. But the very things that prompt we survivors of sexual abuse to see ourselves as different, perhaps as misfits, bring us together in a distinctive community. We constitute a community of people whose different-from-others lives are perfectly normal and expectable for anyone who has suffered what we have experienced. 'Normal' is the most relative of all terms.

Looking honestly at our lives can be painful and hard. Yet there also can be immense freedom in gaining a clearer picture about ourselves. Doing so is important and deeply personal work. It requires time and patience. It is immensely aided by the help of a skilled and trusted helper, whether a friend or a therapist. Personally, I cannot imagine any better place in which to pursue this work than with someone who has the knowledge, skills, and experience to help me maximize the gain from my efforts.

It may be true that no one knows us better than we know ourselves. At the same time, others see us in ways we don't—and can't—see ourselves. Using their observations can deepen our insight into our own lives. I think there is immense profit in figuring out what our own 'signs' (i.e., the effects of what we survived) are. But I would caution against become obsessed with this process or in comparing your list with mine or someone else's. The important point is never about *how much* damage we have experienced, but about *where do we go from here?* The goal in perceiving our own pattern of effects must be the same as the ship captain reading the stars: to figure out where we are so we can get where we want to go.

Chapter 7

OF TIME & DISTANCE

Somewhere, Sometime, Over the Rainbow

In dreams of color brightly lit
    she crosses rainbow bridges.
             From Kansas dust to Munchkin mist,
    she rides the wind.

The ribbon strands in muted hues
             tie Kansas plains to Ozian ridges.
    In swirling, girlish disarray,
    she rides the wind.

             A moment mid the Kansas morning,
joined next to one in ruby shoes—
    so swift the changes for one
    who rides the wind.

             But then the days of Oz are past,
the 'bow bent down in mourning.
    The waking kiss in silence asks,
    Who rides the wind?

A Traveler's Advisory

When Dorothy and her companions first glimpse the home of the Wizard of Oz they are standing at the edge of a vast field of poppies. The yellow brick road literally disappears beneath a mat of color. There is perhaps no sight in all of Oz to compare with the one before their eyes. The travelers are seduced by the flowers' gaiety, the brilliant sun in a cloudless blue sky, and the shimmering visage of the distant Emerald City. What they do not know, of course, is that the wicked witch of the West has seeded doom amidst the inviting field of blossoms.

Memories can be like that, inviting but dangerous.

Throughout our journey we have been considering what happens to us as sexual abuse trauma impacts our bodies. We have examined the underlying biology of experience, how trauma affects that, and the very visible consequences of such changes. In this chapter we will continue to look at the consequences of abuse trauma, but we will simultaneously begin to be more concerned about the recovery process. Our focus here is on *memory*. The issues involved in remembering sexual abuse constitute a crossroads where the effects of trauma meet the tasks of recovery.

For many survivors, recovery begins with the craving of remembrances, the desire to reclaim a missing childhood, a wish to confirm or banish lingering ghosts. Why are memories so important? I can tell you that memories go hand in hand with learning, and that both are needed for us to adapt and thrive. Yet such an explanation sounds sterile no matter how factual it might be. Memories matter to us for more personal, emotional reasons.

Memories offer to each of us a sense of personal continuity. Without remembrances a person cannot help but feel disconnected from her or his own self. Whether painful or pleasant, memories reassure us that we exist. They say to us that we are more than a momentary set of urges. They proclaim we belong to a history and a community of people. They fight against our moments of isolation and encourage our hopes for the future. With memories we are people embodying time. Without them we are cast adrift in an endless present.

Many of us who have survived sexual abuse struggle with our memories. No less than anyone else, we covet a full heritage. We want to remember joyous birthday parties and lazy afternoons at the beach. We would be content to remember comforting hugs when home sick from school. But all too often when we reach to the past we encounter . . . blanks. Whether partial or full, these gaps can drive a person crazy. They never fit. They are an itch that cannot be scratched. Or when some memories come, they hang about in shadows, frightening specters that won't allow our eyes to leave them but also won't stand naked and revealed. A desperate sense of isolation, fragmentation, loss, and yearning wrap around the gaps and blurry ghost images.

Then, often when least expected, a memory explodes sharply clear and painful. The shrapnel of buried feelings tears at us from the inside out. But, curiously, we may experience both wholeness *and* devastation in the same moment. There is an 'Aha!' experience—an 'At last I *know.*' And then, in the first timid whispers of these memories to others, there often comes shocked denial and rejection. If the memories are too hard for others to hear about, how easy can they be for us who remember? What we trauma survivors recover is not merely an uncomfortable truth but one our culture wants us to deny in order to 'fit in.' This social pressure diminishes sensitivity to truth and goodness; we resist it and help make our world better by choosing to face and speak hard truths.

But memories can be hard poppies to smell.

How Things Stick—and Why

Just how does Dorothy manage to find her way to return to the Emerald City with the wicked witch's broom? The answer is so obvious no one needs to have it spelled out in the story: she remembers her way back. No map is required save the one in her head. She has learned the path through walking it, and she preserves this learning through her memory.

The ability to remember means we can learn; we don't have to continually reinvent the wheel. Just as we have seen for learning (chapter 3), memory depends upon physical changes in the brain, some of them of short duration and others long-term. While psychobiologists do not yet fully understand the processes of memory, there is widespread agreement on certain basic matters. Short, or 'immediate' memories are thought to be signals sustained in a neural network. Just as a chime when sounded reverberates, continuing the shimmering tone, so the memory persists for a short time as the nerve impulse keeps it coursing along a specific track. For the memory to become more durably stored it must be translated into a chemical compound that can be kept safe for retrieval. Additionally, some structural changes in the nerve cell configuration—specifically, in the transmission patterns between the nerve cells—may also occur. Neuroscientists tell us that our memories are stored as changes in the same brain systems that also participate in our perceptions, our analysis of these perceptions, and our processing of the information we select and save. All of these important functions are intricately spun together into a single web.

But the web is a complex one. We must avoid the mistake of assuming that everything we perceive is neatly deposited, first into immediate memory, then later automatically transferred to long-term storage, where it only requires the right access code to be recovered. Our senses are flooded by stimuli from the outside world. Not all of it is judged by our brain to be of equal importance. The interpretation and cataloging of all this sensory data is an ongoing process. New data can cause us to revisit old, stored material and revise it in light of the new information. Memory in human beings is not exactly like that in a computer. In people, memory—like learning—is a living, dynamic flux. Like a serpentine highway, memory twists and turns through the corridors of our experience, offering us guidance—and sometimes posing puzzling mysteries. To travel through our memories is a circuitous trek along our own yellow brick road.

In the movie version of Dorothy's story, the first glimpse we get of the yellow brick road is in Munchkin Land. It begins in a tiny circular spot that then spirals outward and leads to parts unknown. As Dorothy soon discovers, when she meets Scarecrow, the road forks. In fact, using the yellow brick road one can not only reach the fabled Emerald City, but any other place of importance in the whole of Oz. Although we are not told as much, I suspect that no matter which fork in the road Dorothy takes, she will sooner or later get where she wants to go. In a sense, because the yellow brick can take Dorothy wherever she wants to go, including back to where she has been, it is a circular route. Likewise, healing is 'round about, often seeming to wander, to retrace previously taken steps, and haphazard. Yet, despite how baffling it may seem, the route gets us to where we want to be, if we stay true to our course.

Recall, or Reconstruction--What Are Memories For?

All human beings return to their memories in the context of integrating their hurts and healing their wounds. Remembering is not just the reenactment of old pictures, but the selective fishing out of particular details and the partly conscious, partly unconscious reframing of these details in revised interpretive schemes. The recall of memories is not for the sake of record keeping but for the end of finding *meaning*. Like the traveler consulting a map, the significance is in seeing where we have been to better understand where we are and get a sense of how to move toward where we want to be. Memories are dynamically reconstructed to facilitate a sense of direction and movement.

We do this creative work again and again and again. I do not mean to suggest we play unfairly with our memories, nor that we can never trust what we or anyone else remembers because of the distorting effect occurring whenever we recall something. In fact, the general reliability of our memories is what sustains our confidence that we have indeed learned something. Nevertheless, we do *use* our memories, so they need not hold us helplessly captive. We can trust our memories to the extent we understand their nature.

Oz can help us understand this process. Let us imagine what might go through Lion's mind when, upon the return to the Emerald City, he has a moment to reflect back on the quest to gain the wicked witch's broom. Doubtless he remembers a rush of images mirroring the places and events themselves: the dark shadows of the haunted forest, the attack of the flying monkeys, the search for Dorothy, the tussle with the castle guards, the infiltration of the witch's fortress, the rescue of Dorothy, the entrapment of himself and his companions, and the final showdown with the wicked witch. Accompanying these images are re-experienced feeling tones: his reluctance to enter the forest, his terror at the suggestion of ghosts ("I *do* believe in ghosts . . . I *do* believe in ghosts!"), the surge of adrenaline while fighting the palace guard, the sensation within the castle of being trapped. There are so many things to remember—and more than one way to assess the memories.

Lion could revert to his old patterns, dwelling on his cowardly moments: the humiliation of being forcibly picked up by Scarecrow and Tin Woodsman when he begins to run away, his asking to remain behind, and other moments of natural fear. After all, he has conditioned himself to focus on these details and he has accustomed himself to using these details to reinforce his low self-esteem. But his experiences with Dorothy have changed him. Lion is no longer the *Cowardly* Lion when they return to the Emerald City. He may recall his feelings, but he also can rely upon his remembrance of acts of bravery. He may have felt like running away, but what he did was stay and fight. A hallmark of health is the ability to manipulate our remembering so as to highlight what promotes integration of the whole into our quest for health.

I don't mean we need to make up memories. The whole notion of false memories plagues the field as it is. The reality of memory is that all memories are *re-creations* rather than mere *recollections*. What we want to do in understanding this nature of memory is utilize it to advance our progress through life. When we recover memories of abuse we need a purpose in mind. We need to intend memory recovery as part of our larger recovery effort. Like the traveler pulling out the map, the recall of memories should be to fix our location, then to help us better see where we are now and where we are going.

We can profit from being aware of something else too. Because memory, learning, and reflection are closely intertwined realities, it is more a theoretical distinction than a practical one about when each is happening. Do we remember what we want to, or do we remember *everything*, but only choose to admit certain portions? Do our interpretations and reinterpretations actually change our memories, or influence what gets fetched out of storage? I think ultimately these interesting questions are quite secondary to another query: *Do we remember so as to hurt or to help ourselves?* The healthy use of memories promotes realistic adaptation to facilitate life and growth.

The reworking of memories is not a one-time adventure. We return to our memories countless times each day, and some are obviously more significant for us than others. The experience of life is never so straightforward as we might imagine it. Every day things happen that remind us of previous happenings. We draw upon our memories to place today's events in a perspective continuous with the past. To some degree, this is seeing the present through the lens of the past. But we also see the past through the present. Rather than linear in nature, engaging memories is a nonlinear and frequently circular process.

False Creations?

But if remembering is reconstructing, then isn't it possible that false memories can be made? Indeed it is possible—the very nature of memory makes it possible. The shifting that occurs in memory is normal and happens to everyone, though very few of us ever consider the phenomenon and hardly anyone ever has any reason to be upset by it. The shifts are generally gradual, minor, and over time. Yet false memories do occur.

A significant body of research has substantiated not only the reality of false memories but that they are not particularly difficult to create. The worry in treating clients is that a therapist, like the bumbling wizard, will resort to flash and mirrors and unwittingly add to the client's problems. The power of suggestion is potent and when it comes from a trusted figure it grows even more powerful. When a condition results from the suggestion of a physician or therapist it is called *iatrogenic* (Greek for 'healer created'). A false memory created in response to a professional helper's suggestion is an iatrogenically induced memory.

But how much of a concern should this be? Though I have no doubt that some of us have been victimized by memories of a victimization that never happened, I also have no doubt that this happens far less often than some imagine. I also know this: a therapist who spends more time playing detective than healer is wasting a client's time. The bottom line is simple: as professionals show restraint and respect to follow where their clients lead them, then we who seek help can trust them—and our memories, however small or great, many or few. In the final analysis, it is not the past that brought us to therapy but our troubles in the present. Those troubles need to be the focus, not the mystery of what might have elicited them when such an issue is in doubt.

False memories can also be built on genuine events. As we've discussed, memories are not fixed, static things. They change somewhat with every recall, because they are brought up by new contexts to which they adapt. A neuroscientist might say they are consolidated over time; what we need to grasp is that every time they surface they are being reworked. It is possible, for example, that the remembrance of an innocent event, such as having our genitals touched during bathing, can become a root to the later elaboration of an abuse fantasy. How can such a momentous transformation occur? The weight of culture impresses upon us the private, special status of certain body parts. We may come to associate both shame and guilt with our genitals. The simple felt memory of the sensation of being touched may, under these influences, grow into an imagined event where we were violated.

It is impossible to know how often such things happen. But we do know how awful and how common the reality of sexual abuse is. We need hardly resort to explaining away memories of abuse as the products of fantasy when we have so much evidence of the pandemic prevalence of such violations. I will reiterate a point made before: it is not the professional's task to prove or disprove the factual foundation of an abuse report or memory. Instead, the task is to aid in healing, which requires respect and trust of the client if it is to be given in return.

As we have seen already, healing is a circular process, with the retracing of our steps again and again. As memories surface and are revisited they may grow, shift subtly, or change in unexpected directions in either content or feeling tone. We may come to acutely question our sanity in the midst of all this. But does this internal agony suggest that our abuse memories are false? Are they really just fantasies?

I doubt I am alone in having asked how real my fragmentary memories are. However, I see no motive for me—or anyone else—to create such disturbing, unhappy, terrible images. And I certainly have experienced long years of struggle and pain. Still, I can't help but wonder at times if the memories are accidental fantasies, the products of a desperate wish to make sense of a chaotic life. On the other hand, even if they are, it makes my pain no less nor my journey less important. I may never know for certain. But over the years I have become content to rely on *as if* thinking. Treating my memories *as if* they reflect reality is

76

reasonable and helpful. So, doubt if you must, but do not permit those doubts to keep you off the road you must build and walk.

Perhaps most often the problem is not that a memory is false but that it is so horrid we don't want to believe it is accurate. The broken bits and pieces make it easier to handle the horror, but they also invite our doubts. We can't help but ask, 'If this really happened, and was so horrible, how could I not remember it for a time?' But another query is just as valid: 'How could I possibly keep in mind anything that terrible? I don't *want* to remember it!'

We protect ourselves from the handicap of having to live with a terror too heavy to carry every day. After years of lugging around all this baggage, though, a veil lifts, the horror peeks out at us, and we question our sanity. The heart of the issue is not if the memory is false, but is it too heavy to carry all at once? As long as it is, the memories come in pieces. First these details are drawn to the forefront; then those emerge. As some surface, others may momentarily fade back a little. The painful remembering we experience represents a normal filtering and reinterpreting process that brings past and present together. The 'truth' lies in the *process*, not the *product*. A whole and entire memory matters less than what we do with what surfaces. And whatever that is merits being accepted every bit as much as we customarily honor anyone other memory.

Can memory be mistaken? Of course it can—for anyone. But that fact does not cause us to doubt other memories and it need not lead us into thinking we should discount abuse memories. To communicate to us that our memories are—or might be—false ones is dishonoring. It becomes another wounding of an already wounded self. No one has that right without compelling evidence and to substantiate the claim and a healing reason to do so.

Digging and Planting

Sexual abuse recovery inevitably involves some working in and through painful memories. It also means rediscovering unexpected remembrances of delight. The past is unearthed like an important archaeological dig, layer by layer, with strata in disarray from the tumultuous earthquakes of the past. That memory of a placid moment before the fire on a midwinter's evening comes out joined with the unspeakable horror of other times before that same hearth. The memories rebirth as second chances, not to get the abuse right, but to confront and own the truth and so become unbound from the chains of trauma.

But memory work, too, is a living process. While we can exercise considerable control over the process, it has its own power, its individual cycles and rhythms, its inescapable moments. We all are experts in our own travels within, yet none of begins with expertise in such traveling. Like Dorothy, we learn by doing.

I have never been quite sure how Dorothy initially finds her way around in Oz. I know she stays to the yellow brick road with single-minded determination. She does have the benefit of inhabitants to guide her, too. But just how much of Oz can Scarecrow have learned hanging up on a stick in a field? I doubt

Cowardly Lion has ventured outside the confines of his forest before joining Dorothy's little band. Tin Woodsman may have traveled previously, but that was obviously awhile ago, since he had stood rusted in place for some time before Dorothy came along, and before that had taken time to build himself a home. Given all this, I imagine that some considerable trial and error is involved in navigating Oz.

Dorothy's explorations are not just a matter of digging out information. They are also efforts at planting seeds of hope. As she explores Oz, learning the lay of the land, she simultaneously forges alliances, discovers new resources within herself, and gains a perspective that ultimately enables her to get where she wants to go. Traveling through Oz is taxing work, often troubling, dangerous, and unpleasant. But the journey also brings many positive encounters. Walking the yellow brick road is how Dorothy *lives* in Oz.

Rooting around among our memories is travel along another yellow brick road. Like the one found in Oz, this path twists and turns. The road crosses fertile ground, soil suited both for digging and for planting. As we access memories we can do more than just sit and suffer the story being told afresh. The soil uncovered, we can now plant seeds of hope. Then, with resolve and confidence, we can resume our walk along the road.

Stuck

I also imagine that Dorothy and friends occasionally find themselves stuck in loops and are left scratching their heads wondering how to get back on track. Abuse survivors get stuck too. The very ability to remember can become a painful reality that we seek to deny or distort as an immediate solution to overwhelming circumstances. It as if we scream out, "Stop! No remembering this!" The reality was bad enough without asking ourselves to face a future of reenactments.

But our bodies remember. They must remember. The biological impact is too real, the alterations too significant, not to be stored in the body. The body must find ways to accommodate to the reality our consciousness shrinks from. A counselor might refer to 'repression,' but the body never forgets, nor represses. The body works with what it has experienced, as best it can, with or without the mind's help. Perhaps each body memory reflects itself to some degree in our body postures and mannerisms, the way we hold ourselves when afraid or angry, the way we move when anxious or excited.

If the body cannot find the freedom for a time to release these memories through thoughts and words, it must choose other routes, such as muscle tension or immune system weakness. Somehow these memories must have their due, be reworked either consciously or physically. The body knows—we know—that the memories must be integrated before we can move forward. We cannot afford the luxury of remaining stuck.

In Oz, Dorothy reaches a point where she feels truly stuck. The wizard has offered her a way to fly from Oz back to Kansas. This solution appeals to her. But Toto jumps from the box beneath the balloon and Dorothy goes after him. The choice costs her the flight and she is left to watch as the wizard drifts away.

Yet what seems in the moment a disappointment proves to be a benefit. By not leaving Oz through flight, Dorothy is able to finally realize her own power to return herself to Kansas. We all encounter many chances to take flight in life. These opportunities may hold immense appeal. We may not consider that flying away from where we are may mean leaving behind important parts of ourselves, or our potential.

Two particularly important temptations face those of us who survive sexual abuse. Especially when we have such painful experiences early in life, our response to trauma may be one or another kind of flight. Essentially, we may seek escape by time travel, or by movement through space. Both are extreme measures of escape from a situation where bodily escape is impossible. Time travel, as a flight *from* time, will occupy us here; next chapter we will consider another kind of escape through time as well as that through space.

The consciousness of human beings has a marvelous, truly magical ability to *pretend*. The conscious mind can act *as if* an event has not happened. By fleeing from time, the consciousness removes from itself any contents it experiences as too threatening. It simply 'forgets' them. *Repression* is the term used for forcing into unconsciousness materials consciousness cannot bear.

Sigmund Freud, the father of psychoanalysis, understood how critical repression is to trauma. Although he has been criticized for allegedly minimizing the incidence of sexual abuse, his recognition of its awful reality exists throughout his writings. In almost the last thing he wrote, his *An Outline of Psycho-Analysis,* Freud pointed to the reality of sexual abuse of children not only by adults but also by other children (often brothers or sisters)—things he termed "common enough"—as an example of the truth that the events of early years are of "paramount importance" for the whole of later life. Freud comprehended that a child's impressions of what takes place might be subjected to repression either immediately or at the time the impressions seek to return as memories. Such repression, he warranted, prompts a variety of detrimental long-term consequences. In his *A General Introduction to Psychoanalysis,* Freud explained that repression is "the essential preliminary condition" for the later development of symptoms.

I won't go into the debate over the exact nature and extent of repression. It is enough to note that the history of the study and treatment of sexual abuse trauma has concerned itself mightily with a reality this term seems best to encompass. As a general rule, clinicians working with trauma survivors agree on certain things. They agree, for example, that some repression is normal and that everyone represses some things—even Dorothy. The magical transition back to

Kansas almost has the feel of a cloud of repression settling in as Dorothy struggles to remember what only moments ago was so clear and forceful.

But they also agree that the kind of repression we are concerned with here eventually becomes a source of trouble, the root of many rotten fruits. How is this condition to be undone? Freud, in the just mentioned *General Introduction,* offered the hope that making the unconscious conscious will relieve the repression and thereby undo the conditions under which symptoms arise. What is left is something more easily managed—a conflict within that can be identified and dealt with effectively. Freud equated the removing of repressions with the filling in of gaps in the memory. By recovering the memories, which insist on expression one way or another, the person is free to leave behind the dysfunctional symptoms that plague her or his life.

Two Triggers and the Blast from the Past

Recovery often begins with an awakened awareness. What is that awareness? Typically it is quite simply, "My life isn't working." Or perhaps we might phrase it, "I'm not getting anywhere!" The same sentiments are true in Oz. Scarecrow, Tin Woodsman, and Lion all come to such awareness with Dorothy's advent in their lives. She triggers a change in each of them. For those of us in the Kansas of trauma survival, this awareness may come suddenly or slowly. The veil of repression may be suddenly punctured, or only slowly lift as we begin to recover memories.

There are many ideas about how we may recover memories associated with the experience of trauma. I find one theory, known as the 'two trigger theory,' to be very useful. In essence, it says simply this: traumatic memories are recovered when two triggers are pulled. The first trigger is the presence of something in the immediate environment that is associated unconsciously with the abuse trauma. The second trigger is *safety.* When the latter trigger is pulled in the presence of the first, then the first trigger is able to fetch at least that part of the trauma associated with that triggering stimulus.

Somehow we know when it has become safe enough to let the trauma we have been holding come out of the darkness into the light. This experience, like so many others encountered by survivors, is a mixed one. On the one hand, it may feel like a kind of rebirth. In fact, we may describe it in terms more usually associated with a religious conversion, a kind of 'being born again' that brings with it a sense that life is just starting. On the other hand, both triggers being squeezed, we may feel blown away. Like a tidal wave, what comes bursting out may threaten to sweep us away. (This latter reality is further addressed in a moment.)

Memories may surface in unexpected ways. Some find that what later emerges as a full-fledged memory first had expression in a dream image. Is Dorothy's journey to Oz just a silly dream? Or might it be a dream filled with memory pieces? The latter seems a possibility when we hear Dorothy excitedly pointing to the three farmhands and Professor Marvel and proclaiming that the four of them had all been in Oz with her. What is Dorothy trying to remember in a dream of Oz?

Our biology is such that dreams are able to draw, from long-term memory storage, pieces left from very early incidents. Is Dorothy finding through her dream of Oz a way to slay the wicked witches of her earliest years? Psychologists know that it is in dreams that sometimes we weave into being earlier experiences, events too frightening to face except in the disguise of a dream with all its alterations, and then only when we have enough distance from the event and enough strength to let them resurface.

These memories seem to be recovered in the same two-trigger fashion. Something during the day, something associated unconsciously with the abuse, sticks until the safety of a dream liberates it. Dorothy's dream incorporates her experience of the farmhands, each cast according to type, and many other people and incidents. All can come safely together in her dreams and be worked toward a successful resolution of what eludes her conscious grasp. Dreams are safe because our conscious mind can pretend they are only fictions. This *as if* process is as natural as a night's sleep. By this pretense consciousness can give the unconscious the liberty to disgorge potentially threatening materials.

In all of this the body is striving to heal itself.

Swimming in Pain

We will do well to pay attention not merely to our body needs, but to its messages. Patience is a must. Recovery is a *process*—not a product. It tends to happen bit by bit. A memory here and there is interspersed with new insights, flashes of feeling, and changes in how we feel physically. It is important that we treat ourselves kindly. Remembering that the memories are in the body, and may very well be explicitly embodied in physical sensations as recall occurs, it is essential to reverence the body, acting deferentially to its needs at such times. If nothing else, at such periods it is especially important to grant one's self adequate nutrition, rest, and playful exercise.

Accompanying our conscious experiencing of abuse memories may be body memories in the form of specific sensations originally paired with the abuse experience. For example, we might find ourselves feeling unexpected body aches. There might be either numbing or tingling sensations. We might feel pain in some specific area that we can't explain by illness or injury. Any new or unexpected physical sensation is worth considering as an accompaniment of the recovery of memory, but especially so those that suddenly appear in critical spots like limbs (perhaps injured while trying to fend off the abuser), or mouth (perhaps gagged or forced to engage in sexual acts), or genital areas. The body speaks eloquently, but we must be prepared to learn its signals and give them a respectful hearing. Though alarming, such body sensations have their role in recovery. Obviously, distressing physical symptoms are worth checking out for other possible causes, too, but if nothing is discovered, don't discount the possibility of what we have been discussing.

If this sounds like hard work, it is because the work *is* hard. It can also be dangerous.

Caution!

If Dorothy's seemingly innocuous dream of Oz isn't safe to be paraded in the daylight, how safe can a memory of abuse be? The process of recalling memories, particularly when they happen a little at a time can be very anxiety provoking. The memories may feel unreal, almost like they belong to someone else. If they seem hard to us to believe, who else is likely to credit them if we tell? To remember is threatening enough, but to remember *and not be believed* is devastation incarnate. Who can easily risk that?

Retrieving memories can constitute one of the more dangerous stretches of the yellow brick road. A whole host of feelings can swirl around the experience: shame, disgust, self-loathing, terrifying rage, horror, abject despair, paralyzing fear. The brightness of the day can be swallowed in the grave of the blackest night of the past. In such circumstances it is easy enough to despair of the journey and forsake the road. We may hide in Lion's woods, crawl into Tin Woodman's cottage, or hang ourselves beside Scarecrow. But we don't provide ourselves by woods, cottages or cornfields apart from the ones who call them home. In trying times, when the journey is in peril, the safety and warmth provided by trusted traveling companions is essential. Every one of us engaged in such work needs alongside us the sensibility of Scarecrow, the empathy of Tin Woodsman, and the courage of Lion.

Yet every survivor's experience in this regard is fully unique. In all this talk of recovering memories we are yet to reckon fully with another possibility: such recovery may never be full, or happen at all! This work is not graded; there is no pass-fail. We remember what we remember. If we make remembering too important, we get in our own way. It is like focusing on how to get to Oz so completely we forget to actually go there, or having reached the fabled city forget why we came. The ultimate goal is not the Emerald City but *home*.

We survivors often struggle to have self-respect. An inability, or just slowness to remember, may be self-interpreted as another abject failure in a long life of losing ventures. But Dorothy, Scarecrow, Tin Woodsman, and Lion all faced many moments of weakness, failure of nerve, and undesired outcomes. Life carries no guarantees even when we play by the rules and do the very best possible. The healing of memories requires a willingness to settle for whatever the body yields up as enough—at least for now. The pressure to remember more likely will block memories rather than free them.

Just as Dorothy walks the twisting yellow brick road, so might we travel the labyrinths of memory. As we do we shall rehearse the lessons of the past, but we can also integrate them into the present. Like Dorothy, who found that she belongs to both Kansas and Oz, we belong to past and present, to memories and possibilities. We may not be able to choose our citizenship, but we can choose how we will live as citizens.

Chapter 8

Acting Out, Growing Up & Going Away

Up, Up, and Away!

Leaving home is hard at any age.

I want to kick up my heels and fly!
Get me *out* of here!

Goodbye Kansas, hello Oz.

I know I can go as far as my rage
Will take me and I intend to try

Flying over the rainbow.

Wanting to Be Well

We all want to be well, not only in our memories, but in every other respect. As we have seen—and too many of us have experienced—sexual abuse is adverse to health, affecting body processes in ways that mean short-term adaptations often purchased at the price of acquiring long-term disadvantages. Thus our boundaries respond to trauma so as to preserve our inner selves as best they can, but the result can mean problems over time. Our minds flee from the time of the abuse, leaving memories hidden behind a veil of horror to great to face—for now. But life is a matter of stretching and reaching toward growth. Every contraction and retreat must be seen as a prelude to renewed efforts to live and prosper.

While we gather ourselves, our bodies continue to function, coping as best they can with our experiences. Remarkably, we manage imaginatively and hopefully. Even extreme responses reflect creativity and hope. What is important to us is grasping that our bodies are speaking a language of their own. Body symptoms can be called metaphorical in that they speak *as if* something is one thing, when in fact it is another. Our body pain may shout at us that we are still being victimized, even though the actual physical acts are long done. We may even talk metaphorically about what we feel in the body, saying for instance, "I feel as if I'm broken." But whether we use words or not, our bodies speak.

Sexual abuse survivors speak in and through the flesh even when their voices have been muted and their memories kept hidden away. We may think readily of this 'talking' as those medical problems the doctors can find no cause for. Though real to us, they seem less real, or unreal, to others. From the very start such body messages have a purpose, and it is an important one.

Even before we are ready to act on it, our bodies cry out for help. We all have an instinct for health. It is an inevitable accompaniment to the nature of life. No one chooses illness willingly. Trauma has to be expressed, though, and if it cannot gain access to the outside world in any other manner it will do so through manifest physical illness. If the lips cannot utter a sound, the skin may speak eloquently in allergic reactions. If the head cannot bring forth images to speak, it may produce headaches to talk about. If the sinking sensation in the stomach cannot find release in vocalization it may express itself in gastrointestinal distress. But be sure of this: *One way or another, trauma will speak.*

Dorothy and her companions spare themselves many troubles when they release their internal pressure by talking to each other, by joining arm-in-arm as they walk the yellow brick road, and by hugging and crying when the circumstances warrant it. These activities mitigate the impact of the traumatic events they encounter. They permit Dorothy and her friends to integrate their experiences and grow. As a result, they emerge healthy at the end of their journey.

But complete health is often an elusive condition for survivors of sexual abuse. Boundary violations have opened up gaping holes through which the energy of life is dissipated. Patterns of long-term effects have produced chaotic efforts at growing, as though a tree twisted this way and that, with little success, to reach the sunlight and warmth it requires to prosper. Yet human beings are persistent. We sexual abuse survivors—because we have to be—are remarkably tenacious. As a therapist working with survivors I echo what many of my colleagues have expressed: sexual abuse survivors are unsurpassed in the courage and grace they often show despite the most horrific of life experiences.

If we are denied the normal quality of life and health we might have enjoyed, we nevertheless possess a *relative* measure of health. It is too easy—and misleading—to focus on deficits. What remains may not work as well as would like, but it keeps us in the game of life. As such, hope springs eternal. Every cry for help has the possibility of being answered. While we wait, we struggle on, doing the best we can.

Hiding from the Body

In fact, we do the best we can all along. It starts in the midst of the trauma itself. As seen last chapter, the consciousness of human beings has a marvelous, truly magical ability to *pretend*. The conscious mind can act *as if* the body is not present. By fleeing in space, our consciousness detaches itself from distressing body sensations, from feelings that are unbearable. Consciousness takes up a new location, one safely removed from the distressing sensations.

Dissociation, a breaking apart of experience, provides us a way of fleeing through space. I earlier alluded to the possible interpretation of Dorothy's experience as a dissociative one. When one place is too painful for the consciousness to inhabit, it removes itself to somewhere else. Or, when an experience is overwhelming, it can be made manageable by breaking it into smaller, discrete portions. Dissociation can refer to either the process of disconnecting, or to one of partitioning.

In the latter case, the most extreme form of dissociation is seen in *dissociative identity disorder* (DID; formerly termed 'multiple personality disorder'). In this condition, the person manages the parts of experiences, including their feeling tones, by maintaining separate personalities. This rare condition is almost exclusively associated with early, severe and prolonged child abuse. As in every other form of dissociation, the goal in healing is the reintegration and reconnecting of the pieces into the whole.

Unfortunately, though dissociation of one degree or another is a relatively common phenomena, its occurrence is facilitated by our culture's acceptance of a dualist philosophy. *Dualism* teaches that we are *not* our bodies. Instead, we inhabit our bodies temporarily; our true—or 'essential' self—is something termed variously the 'soul' or 'spirit.' Such a distinction, with its explicit degrading of the body, has a host of unfortunate consequences, one of which is encouraging dissociation, which also has its roots in the body's biology.

C. G. Jung, the founder of analytic psychology, offered a foundational piece of corrective advice. In a letter, Jung urged his reader to realize that the self always has been and always will be both our center and our boundaries. It can be harmed, perhaps even broken into discrete pieces, but it *cannot* be removed. In healing, the self experiences itself fully only when it does so *wholly*.

To heal we must seek wholeness, and to seek wholeness we must rejoin body and mind. Our consciousness must re-inhabit the body in full, accepting the weight of the pain it has experienced and stored. We must reawaken to our responsibility to inhabit the place which is our body—this happened to *me!*—and find a way to live in the present, connected to the past, but walking toward the future. Hiding from the body can only be a temporary solution. Somehow we must remember how to be in our bodies again.

Stuck Again

If learning depends on memories—things sticking—then continued growth depends upon not getting stuck or getting unstuck. Unfortunately, trauma, by its wounding capability, arrests our body's attention, drawing the focus of our natural energies to bear on trying to heal the hurt. This focal point slows, perhaps stops our normal, expected development. And so we become stuck.

We may be stuck in our life development because of a frustrating loss of memories, or we may be stuck in the memories themselves. Yet there is more.

Being stuck, as a fixation at one point, affects our progress at other points. With our attention and energy focused at one thing, everything else is deprived of the care and devotion it might otherwise receive. Like a net, pulling on a single cord draws back the entire net. The disruption caused by trauma means some aspects of childhood are never properly developed. They become another part of our losses.

We may talk about a 'loss of innocence,' or simply wonder what it must be like to have had a 'normal' childhood. For survivors of childhood sexual abuse a dastardly double bind is common. At the same time we are held back in some respects, we are thrust forward in others. Unready, unprepared, and unwilling we are forced into roles and acts reserved more properly to adulthood. The effort to adapt draws energy, and that is energy at the expense of how it would otherwise be employed. In effect, sexual abuse requires we grow up while simultaneously preventing it.

Now, no one chooses to get stuck in trauma, anymore than Dorothy chooses to get stuck in Oz. But extreme situations in a hostile environment require extreme measures. These measures are drawn from a child's—not an adult's—repertoire. Because they work—the child survives—they are extremely self-reinforcing. We may come to rely on childish measures well into adulthood, even though they no longer serve the same purpose or have as adaptive an outcome.

Retreat and Advance!

If we must give up our childish defenses, at least let us honor them. Though inappropriate for an adult, they were perfectly suited to keeping us together during the years when childhood was being stolen. We had to retreat to advance. Life, faced with death, gave us an out.

Perhaps all of life is of the nonlinear nature we found true of memory. The child may be father to the man, but it seems just as true that in every grandmother lurks a little girl eager to come out and play. The seasons of life, no less than those in the world around us, are not monoliths of a singular nature. Spring strains beneath the Winter's frozen ground and Summer's heat recalls the barrenness of snow-covered fields. Life loops around and through us like vines in their circuitous journey around a telephone pole. The very essence of growth is a parade of second chances. Life never tires of trying to heal.

Recovery from sexual abuse is a living process. It commences with the abuse itself. Already, in the moment the trauma wounds us, the body has mobilized its resources to minimize the damage and initiate the healing. When a person formally enters into a commitment to recover from the abuse trauma, a contract is entered into to work with the body's own natural, ongoing efforts. In the truest sense, recovery is becoming and being the self *at last*. No longer is the body set against itself; now it is fully supported in healthy ways of striving to be whole. The extreme coping responses required in the trauma can finally be put to rest as the body is supported in leaving the past and coming into the present.

Up until fairly recently, a survivor of abuse who talked about past trauma could expect to be told, "Grow up! Put the past behind you and move on!" The advice is not nearly so bad as it is heartless. It makes what any survivor wants—growth—sound easy, and suggests that the past is something casually set aside. Perhaps, slowly, things are changing in our society. A new appreciation for the biological basis of traumatic changes sees the damage to developing persons. There are encouraging signs that today's health professionals are finally wakening to the insight that Freud had more than a century ago—that abuse can and does play out in the body as well as the mind, in life development as well as in particular experiences.

Still, there remain many like Auntie Em. Her answer to Dorothy is simply, "we all dream silly things." Dorothy gets the message and at once defers to her caretaker. Like Dorothy, some of us remain unbelieved when we talk of past trauma. But some of us are listened to, our lives reappraised in light of new, terrible knowledge. For some of us, the price we paid in our development is at last acknowledged.

I wonder what Dorothy's life before Oz was really like. What happened to her mother and father? Why is she with Auntie Em and Uncle Henry, who seem old enough to be her grandparents? Was she taken from her parents for some reason? Does she carry an unspeakable family secret? In the movie version familiar to most of us these questions never surface. They remain subliminally implied in the very terms of address: *Auntie* Em and *Uncle* Henry. But her behavior gives some clues that not all has been rosy. She is quick to assume blame for herself, is overly apologetic, and quickly embraces running away as the solution to her problems. That she has tendencies to be a caretaker seems likely in her response to Professor Marvel's suggestion that her aunt is suffering because of Dorothy's absence. Yet Dorothy's past remains an enigma.

One matter is as certain for Dorothy as for any other child. Children bruise as easily as young fruit on the branch or vine. Or, to use another metaphor, as a stone into any pond will bring ripples, the smaller the pond the more appreciable the disturbance. The younger we are, the more pronounced may be the total effect of trauma. To return to our first metaphor, a blight while a plant is first forming will redirect the growth in ways that the same disease in a mature plant will not. In sum, the younger we are when the wounds begin, the greater the potential disruption to our development.

As we have learned earlier in our journey, the road of development—both body and mind—is paved by experiences that affect us at the level of our brain cells and work themselves out into the very structure of our personality. A benign environment affords greater opportunity for normal, expected development. A hostile environment breeds the very aggression that spawns it. We all enter the world with potential that awaits an environment to nurture it or frustrate it. To realize our full potential we *must* have support. That is a big condition to be met and one a child has no control over. No matter how strong the child's biological constituency, a deplorable environment can wear away the defenses of health and inflict deep wounds.

The scars linger. They are easily torn open to bleed again. Long after the abuse has stopped, even mundane, quite ordinary events can scratch and tear at old wounds. Suddenly, there is bleeding again, and pain. We can pretend, but there is no complete substitute for what we have lost. We can hide, but reality always finds us out.

Is this what happens to Dorothy in Oz? Of course, normal in Oz is extraordinary in Kansas, but leaving that aside for the moment, does Dorothy's behavior reveal impairments? Perhaps so, if we reckon the glimpses of immaturity that peek through the remarkably adult demeanor that Dorothy so often musters. But I do not want to be too hard on Dorothy; she is of an age where maturity and childishness vie naturally for prominence. I prefer to see her as a remarkably resilient young woman who intuitively pursues the things that allow her to not merely survive Oz but to actually thrive there.

Being stuck developmentally means having some areas of personal functioning that don't work well in the present because they belong to the past. A twelve year old who retains five year old functioning in an area is going to be perceived not merely as immature, but as maladapted. It is important to note, though, that developmental sticking points are almost always just that: points, or perhaps even limited patterns, but not pervasive, across-the-board regressions. Rarely do any of us collapse into a psychological fetal position. We survivors, like Dorothy, are made of sterner stuff.

Yet children are not adults in miniature, and their responses, as well as their capabilities, differ from adults. Let's return to learning and memory for a moment. Children, especially the very young ones, process experience somewhat differently from adults. On the one hand, in the first years of life the storage of memories varies from the process in an adult. A preverbal child's memories are not easily accessible to the adult's verbal-dependent way of operating. The memories adults have of the preverbal period are few, difficult to access, and elude verbal expression. Brain connections are still forming in the early years, and as we shall presently see, this can have a pronounced influence on later life. On the other hand, the dependence of children on images has both advantages and liabilities.

In infancy and early childhood the brain is still maturing and some of the communication connections between the left and right halves of the brain are not yet fully formed. A large band of fibers that joins the two hemispheres, called the corpus callosum (from Latin words that picture it as a 'body of hardened skin'), takes time to grow into its role. Before the age of four, children's perceptions are stored in both hemispheres but may remain unlinked. Thus an event that creates a complex set of signals, especially mixed or ambiguous signals, is broken into separate memories in accordance with the character of each half of the brain. For example, the left hemisphere may code into memory the words "I love you," or "You'll thank me for this later." Meanwhile, the right hemisphere is storing feelings of powerlessness, or rage, or shame—all feelings incongruent with the verbal messages in the other hemisphere. The twin set of memories, linked to the same event, but not joined in either their character or connected across the hemispheres, remain discrete and troubling. Later in life, the person may be deeply disturbed by the incongruity.

Children also are less linear and more dependent on discrete images. Their inner world is populated by memories that seem more like artistic still frames than a moving picture. As they enter the school years, the images link together to form a continuous story line, though early on it is one relatively devoid of marked differences between peaks and valleys. Still later, the story fleshes itself into full-fledged drama, with distinctions sharply drawn between the players and circumstances. A note of, and tolerance for, ambiguity can begin to be glimpsed. In adolescence, the drama takes on mythic character as the young person may wrap around herself or himself a larger-than-life persona. During these years the child will often travel in the company of associates whose collective energy goes into forming the distinctive labels by which they are known to each other (e.g., 'jock,' 'dweeb,' etc.).

Imagine That!

Throughout this long developmental processing of experience one thread remains constant: *imagination*. It is this fact that was seized upon by some psychological thinkers who erred in giving too much weight to the child's generation of fantasy. Though imagination and fantasy are important to all human beings, and especially to children, that fact in no way should suggest that what a child reports as reality is inevitably or even generally just the consequence of an overactive imagination. False reports of child abuse by children are almost always prompted by adult coaching. Why would a child want to imagine something like sexual abuse?

Instead, we should see imagination as indelibly human. Imagination, using metaphors and stories, is what we do to put things together, hold on to them, and give them meaning. Early in life we creatively form and hold images. As we learn language we tell stories.

There may be some benefits to depending so much on images. This may be a more holistic, if nonlinear way of experiencing. It may lend itself to a better integration among event, feeling, and reflection. The increase of verbal skills comes at a price, the loss of close affiliation with the nonverbal parts of self and experience. As we grow out of our childhood years we may encounter difficulty reconnecting to our less verbally dependent experiences. However, as I am suggesting in this book, metaphors and stories can serve as bridges between language and the body, between early nonverbal experiences and later verbal ones.

Interestingly, children are more active than adults in the production of metaphors, both of 'appropriate' and 'inappropriate' ones by adult standards. Apparently, the ability and desire to generate metaphors is not a matter of age or education; preschool children outperform college students, as at least one research study has shown. Unhappily, as children grow older they become more infected by adult linearity and literality. At least by the time we are in primary grades we seem to get quite clearly the message that *as if* thinking is inferior thinking.

Maybe we need to retreat in order to advance. Just as we may have done so in development to cope with our trauma, perhaps now we can intentionally and intelligently draw upon earlier ways of handling life to help us be 'grown up.' We do not have to be infantile to benefit from being childlike. We may have lost our innocence too early, but perhaps we can reclaim a measure of it through metaphors. Maybe that is the real door through which our inner child awaits us.

Metaphors may prove to have astonishing abilities to release materials stored in the body by embodying them in language. At any rate, metaphors appear to be appropriate and useful tools to assist the processing of experience at any age. We survivors of sexual abuse, no matter our age, may benefit from finding or developing appropriate metaphors to connect our past experiences with a present empowerment. Attending carefully to Dorothy's story may mean attaching ourselves to her success, thereby finding our own ways to succeed.

How Do We Move On?

But let us pause to sum up these ideas about development. Abuse trauma can produce developmental problems, leaving survivors stuck. These sticking points are not divorced from memory, but in fact are connected closely to learning, memory, and the way people process experience. They may reveal themselves in the course of ordinary events but are especially likely to show up under mounting stress. Unfortunately, if predictably, when left unaddressed in childhood the sticking points collect more and more garbage to be dealt with in adulthood.

Therapists who work with survivors are accustomed to seeing a familiar pattern. After striking out on a life of one's own there is a flurry of attention given to new demands, new opportunities, new challenges. But sooner or later, things begin to settle down. New friends have been made, a new family perhaps formed. And in the midst of catching one's breath, a sudden tightness shows itself, a thorny knot inside that leaves the survivor feeling dizzy.

I wonder how often Dorothy felt that way. She ran away from home, ended up in Oz—and got stuck. I wonder how much drag Kansas was on her as she walked through Oz. Though she had left Kansas, she really had not left her problems. Oz adds new ones. Stress mounts. The little irritants grow larger, often way beyond their actual importance. And then, at some point, may come the straw that breaks the camel's back—or the fire that threatens to burn up the strawy Scarecrow.

Almost inevitably, as we grow older, the pressures mount upon us to resolve the stuck points. The accumulating weight of unfinished business is like a ledger with past due bills that keep adding interest and penalties. We may put off facing the total but our credit is exhausted and the collectors keep piling on the pressure. No wonder so many of us find that growing up is often circum-vented by simply going away, taking our childhood sticking points with us.

Things can reach such a point because we can become so incredibly stuck. Now, none of us chooses to get stuck in trauma, or in a childish defense or way of functioning, anymore than Dorothy chooses to get stuck in Oz. But extreme situations in a hostile environment can call forth extreme measures. These measures are drawn from a child's—not an adult's—repertoire. The child's re-sources are limited, yet often startlingly effective. Because they work—the child survives—they are extremely self-reinforcing. So we may come to rely on child-ish measures well into adulthood, even though they no longer serve the same purpose or have as adaptive an outcome.

How, then, do we move on? How do we learn to move again? For that mat-ter, given the power of the lessons abuse can teach, how can we learn anything the way we imagine it is meant to be learned? These are tough questions, but not without answers.

The Challenge to the Wounded Self

In another work I once wrote that, "an abused or neglected child is penal-ized on almost every front. . . . They have inadequate parenting models to help them out, they have the normal lack of maturity for their age, they are burdened with traumatic events, and they may need to resort to extreme means to try to protect themselves physically or emotionally, or both." In sum, as I then wrote, "the result is that they may form ways of responding to their situation that help them survive, but cannot be considered optimum choices for healthy develop-ment." The handicaps imposed by sexual abuse trauma pose a challenge to the wounded self: grow through the integration of the hurt, or watch the blood keep ebbing out so that a little more dying happens each day. There is no third alternative. We either grow or wilt. We are living—or dying.

Certainly sexual abuse challenges our sense of self in all its manifold dimen-sions. No less true is how Oz challenges Dorothy. How many of us have ridden tornados, slain not one witch but two, and stared down the fearful visage of a wizard? If Dorothy can grow in the midst of such a world, surely we can prevail in ours. If she can still be sweet Dorothy of Kansas at the end, certainly we can reclaim that sense of self that transforms pain into the celebration of living. It will be no easier for us than it is for Dorothy, but if we want to be where our heart desires, we must take the steps to get there.

The world-renowned developmental psychologist Erik Erikson once re-marked that the key problem of identity is how to sustain a sense of sameness and continuity in the face of our changing fate. What Erikson does not add is a point I wish to emphasize immediately. The self's capacity to maintain a core sense of identity is *never* lost. Developmental retreats are meant to preserve us. Fleeing the body through dissociation likewise intends to preserve our identity. Even in the most extreme dissociative states of multiple personality disorder this core sense is preserved and protected. That sense of self, whole and holy, must be nurtured, encouraged into the sunlight, and allowed once more to grow.

So how do we get unstuck and move on? The terms are relative: we are never so stuck some movement has not been going on already! We can start by appreciating that fact. We can marvel at how we survived. We can look back in order to ready ourselves to move forward. We take stock, give thanks, and pick up a brick. It is time to resume building the road.

Chapter 9

CHANGING RELATIONS

Companions

Dorothy never feels the cold night earth.

Scarecrow's straw beneath suckles her,
seeding dreams that find warming birth
in trusting weddedness of brow to kitty fur.

No coward he whose hide is pillow
to the handmaiden of Kansas
and Princess of Oz!

Tin silent stands his stalwart fellow,
guarding sleeping images of Kansas
beneath the bewitching stars of Oz.

No wonder Dorothy dances in slumbering mirth.

Wounds and Bindings

Dorothy certainly takes her share of lumps in Oz as well as in Kansas. Whether it is the implied violence of Elvira Gulch or the actual mayhem of the wicked witch of the West, there are folk around her bent on doing her harm. Moreover, Dorothy *is* harmed—and not just by the obvious villains. Her hurt begins at home, and although the tornado that sweeps her to Oz most physically represents the trauma Dorothy experiences, it is the rebuffing she finds at home that sets her feet on a dusty Kansas road that ultimately leads to Oz.

All trauma lives up to its name, producing wounds and leaving scars. The seemingly little hurts of Kansas lead up to the big adventure in Oz. Yet, as we saw much earlier, some people prove more resilient than others. I highlighted the biological nature of this quality, but now we must give weight to environmental factors. What are Dorothy's environments in Kansas and in Oz really like? When a person is in a stable, safe, supportive environment, traumatic effects may be substantially mitigated. But, when the relationships surrounding the individual are unhealthy—or worse, abusive—the lack of readily available support can promote developing impoverished internal representations both of the self and of other people. The result is that our fundamental cohesiveness of the self becomes threatened from within. In sum, when we add trauma to the absence of emotional support we get subtraction—the losses we have spoken of at length in our journey together. The extent of trauma's wounding us is intimately related to the strength and health of the bindings available from others.

Although we do not know enough to do more than speculate on most matters about Dorothy's Kansas environment, it seems clear that her support system in Oz proves more rapidly and effectively responsive than her one in Kansas. Let's remember how Dorothy's story opens. She is running toward home, anxiously looking back at some unseen menace. We soon discover that the threat has to do with a rich spinster named Elvira Gulch, who is determined to take Dorothy's dog Toto to the sheriff to have him destroyed.

Dorothy is hopeful that at home she will find the answer to this problem, that her Aunt Em and Uncle Henry will provide for her and Toto both understanding and safety. When she excitedly tries to explain her concern to her aunt and uncle she meets a response pattern that persists throughout the story. Uncle Henry has a sly sense of humor and a manifest passive-resistant style of dealing with conflict. He remains in the shadow of his wife, to whom he continually defers. Aunt Em is a busy woman, focused on the cares of her farm and not amenable to the distractions of an excitable young girl.

As Dorothy tries to tell them about her fears, Uncle Henry stands silent and Aunt Em exasperatedly tells her, "Dorothy, Dorothy, we're busy." Dorothy's shoulders sag in resignation as she leaves to seek the three farmhands. But they also are busy. The only one who interacts with her beyond a quick dismissal confines himself to briefly lecturing her on using her head and avoiding trouble. In her disappointment, Dorothy complains that he simply does not understand.

Then Dorothy does a foolish thing. In what looks to me like an unconscious bid for attention, she puts herself at risk for harm by trying to walk a fence line between two pens filled with massive pigs. Sure enough, her feet become tangled in the wire running along the top and she pitches headfirst amidst the grunting and squealing pigs. But she gets what she has been seeking. Her cries for help finally are heard. A farmhand rushes to her rescue and, at least briefly, Dorothy has an attentive audience.

Immediately, though, Aunt Em bustles over, not to cluck her concern over Dorothy, but to scold the farmhands. Dorothy once more attempts to converse with Aunt Em, who has brought refreshments to the farmhands along with her exhortations for them to be about their work. Once again Dorothy is rebuffed, this time with the words, "Now, Dorothy, just don't be imagining things. You always get yourself into a fret over nothing."

These words introduce a Kansas theme that is repeated even at the movie's end—"There, there, lie quiet now. You just had a bad dream." Dorothy's perceptions are challenged and ultimately rejected by the adults around her. The result is predictable: Dorothy learns not to trust her own perceptions. *Maybe*, she muses, *Oz really was just a dream*. Auntie Em's parting words to Dorothy as she goes back to her chores are, "Find yourself a place where you won't get into any trouble."

Not only are Dorothy's perceptions untrustworthy in her Aunt's eyes, but Dorothy is located as the source of any trouble that might in fact exist. Given such a home environment it seems unlikely Dorothy will be able to avoid trouble. Just as she needed to fall among the pigs to be seen and heard for even a moment, so she must take to the road—and eventually to Oz—to reach a place where her perceptions can be validated, her concerns listened to sympathetically, and her growth encouraged by stalwart, supportive companions.

Now, it is true that Dorothy's aunt and uncle provide for her need for food and shelter. Dorothy can even recall a time when she was sick and her aunt tended to her. Nor are her caretakers completely bereft of caring. After returning from Oz, Dorothy wakes to find herself with Auntie Em sitting beside her, Uncle Henry standing silently in the background. The farmhands crowd in to see her, and even Professor Marvel visits. So Dorothy's environment is not completely absent support, though the emotional support she needs appears to be questionable.

Unfortunately, we know too little about Dorothy's earliest years and the care, or lack of care, she may have received from her natural parents. However, from Dorothy's behavior in both Kansas and in Oz, as well as from what we see in her uncle and—especially—her aunt, certain features of her upbringing seem likely. Her uncle is a relatively passive background figure to his wife, who is stern, often sharp in her words, and rigorously moralistic. Uncle Henry seems benignly unresponsive to Dorothy, while Aunt Em sends mixed messages, attending to Dorothy's obvious physical needs but neglecting her emotional welfare and at times rebuffing her solicitation of emotional support. While Dorothy might be hopeful that her Aunt Em will provide help, she must remain uncertain whether her aunt will be available, responsive, or helpful when called upon.

The support that is such a fundamental aspect of growth is not found by Dorothy in Kansas. She must go to Oz. But note a critical fact: she does not travel alone.

Toto

How easy it is to overlook Toto! Yet at every critical juncture in Dorothy's story, Toto is near the center. Dorothy's world revolves in important ways around her dog. Toto is her Tonto, her ever-faithful companion. He is also her link to home.

On occasion throughout this book I have indicated that we are not alone.

On the other hand, I have emphasized that in many important respects we *are* alone. No one can live my life but me; you are responsible for your life. Each of us has to walk our own road—and we must provide the power for the locomotion that gets us where we desire.

But now we need to widen the circle by looking at the role of our relationships. It is virtually impossible to talk about our wounds without also talking about those who wound us and those who are potential sources of support. Every life story is filled with villains and companions surrounding the central character. Each has a role important to our developing story. A large part of our task is negotiating the plot twists they bring us and learning who we can trust to help us along the way.

But back to Toto. In Dorothy's story, he has an active role. In Kansas, he connects Dorothy to Elvira Gulch, whose wickedness is evident in her hatred of a small dog. In Oz, he is the instrument by which the wicked witch of the west can terrify Dorothy through threatening him harm. How much better off might Dorothy be if she could just let him go! If only she didn't care. But Toto is her lifeline to love and hope.

Consider the situation Dorothy finds herself in. She risks her place in her family, and even her very life, to save this little dog. They are together when the cyclone twists and turns and dumps them in Oz. No wonder she clutches Toto tightly. In an unfamiliar land he is the only soul she knows.

What happens when we find ourselves suddenly cut off from our familiar network of relationships? What happens when we are suddenly alone? Of course, we each handle this in our own way, but we are likely to be influenced in how we react by what it was like for us as a child when this happened. The patterns of relatedness developed during the early years of life shape the response one offers to the new, the unfamiliar, and the isolating aloneness of a life suddenly bereft of support. This is true for Dorothy—and for us.

Those of us who are survivors and those of us who work with them know that adult survivors not only feel isolated, but they often *are* alone. Dorothy is only partially an exception to this common experience. The tornado separates her from Kansas, but she brings a piece of Kansas with her in the person of Toto. This little animal, her constant companion save for those darkest moments in the witch's castle, is more than a faithful friend. Psychologists may point out to us that our penchant for seeking relationship with other people is such that we will do it even if it means accepting substitutes, such as pets, stuffed animals, or cars we give affectionate names. For Dorothy, who knows Uncle Henry will be silently unavailable, and who cannot rely on Auntie Em providing the emotional succor she needs, Toto represents the warmth, love, and unconditional acceptance she cannot find in the adults around her. This condition does not really change in Oz. Her companions, though nominally adults, are not 'human.' They are made of straw, and tin, and kitty fur.

Her attachment to Toto is how Dorothy clings to her aunt and uncle. It seems to me to be of special significance that Dorothy runs away from home after Aunt Em and Uncle Henry's failure to protect Toto from Miss Gulch.

Their abandonment of Toto is a rejection of those qualities of relationship Dorothy has projected unto them through her relationship with the little dog. By severing her attachment to Toto, the adults sever their own attachment from Dorothy. Thus cut loose, what is to prevent Dorothy from running away?

But in Oz, Dorothy must cling to Toto as all she has left of the relationship she has not yet given up on. In fact, in the dark moments of Toto's escape, the vision in the crystal ball in the witch's castle is of a concerned Auntie Em. But when Dorothy cries out, "I'm trying to get home to you, Auntie Em. Oh, Auntie Em, don't go away! Come back! Come back!"—who is she really calling out to? Remember, when the wizard is ready to fly her home to Kansas, Dorothy leaves the safe promise of the air balloon to go after Toto. It is Toto who is clutched tightly in her arms when she first steps out into Oz and when she closes her eyes and clicks her heels to leave Oz.

Toto is the only avenue of reliability open to Dorothy in relating to her aunt and uncle.

Attachment

We may never know what has produced this complex situation for Dorothy, but we can talk meaningfully about the process it represents. Dorothy, like all of us, exists in a web of attachment relationships. This term has come to acquire a particular set of meanings and much significance in modern psychology and warrants our delving a bit into its background. John Bowlby, a British psychologist of the Object Relations school associated with Melanie Klein, who herself was once a young associate of Sigmund Freud, developed over the course of his career a distinctive way of looking at many developmental issues. He elaborated his ideas in what is known as attachment theory. Many others have carried on his work, most notably Mary Ainsworth, but Bowlby's theoretical formulations have remained the hallmark of this way of looking at behavior and relationships. We will profit from attending to his ideas on the subject.

Although Bowlby's definition and description of 'attachment' is easily found in many of his works, I like the formulation he used in a lecture entitled 'The Making and Breaking of Affectional Bonds,' delivered to British psychiatrists in 1976. He explained attachment behavior as efforts to gain and then keep closeness to some individual we desire because we see that person as stronger or wise than our own self, at least in some ways important to us. Such figures provide us a sense of safety from which we can venture out and explore the world. When unwilling separation from them occurs, we experience distress. We feel anxious, perhaps angry. We may develop depression or adopt a kind of emotional detachment. A broken attachment is a serious matter.

In Bowlby's perspective, and as much research confirms, attachment behavior characterizes us from the cradle to the grave. Such behavior persists because it has survival value. It is, in short, biologically rooted in evolutionary development. Interestingly enough, Bowlby said he thought that the most likely function of attachment behavior is found in providing protection. If so, then sexual abuse by its very nature strains attachment because we were not protected from a predator. In a lecture to the American Psychiatric Association on 'Developmental Psychiatry Comes of Age,' delivered a few years before his death, Bowlby speculated that attachment behavior may reflect a biological control system. He saw this residing in the central nervous system and analogous to the physiological control systems that maintain critical life functions, such as blood pressure and body temperature. If true, our attachment system is truly a power to be reckoned with.

The biological rootedness of attachment is nowhere more evident than in the vision of an infant clinging to the mother's breast. But the root picture of bodies joined together remains throughout the life cycle. There is no attachment without closeness. As Bowlby's use of ethological studies illustrate, attachment behavior and patterns are common survival forms in the animal kingdom. Anyone who has visited the primate exhibits at a zoo has seen how monkeys and the great apes cling to one another. But people do likewise. We often miss the attachment qualities inhering to our interactions, such as Dorothy's relation to Toto as a way of relating to her Aunt Em and Uncle Henry. When she attaches to new companions in Oz, she does not do so from a distance, but arm in arm as they skip along the yellow brick road.

Attachments may be broadly distinguished as either *secure* or *insecure*. Bowlby himself identified three principal patterns, although subsequent work has sought to make further distinctions. Of Bowlby's original three patterns, his judgment, as he remarked to American psychiatrists, is that one pattern is consistent with healthy development, and the other two are indicative of disturbed development. The former pattern he termed *secure attachment*. In this pattern, a child meets with available and responsive care. Help is forthcoming when fearful or dangerous situations arise. The child experiences an assurance that the world can be explored because a safety net remains intact to safeguard her or his adventures out into it.

In *anxious resistant attachment* (a pattern exaggerating *dependence*) the care is not reliably available. The caretakers may prove unresponsive or unhelpful when needed. The child acquires not assurance but uncertainty. As a result he or she may cling anxiously to the caretaker and be beset by separation anxiety. Finally, in *anxious avoidant attachment* (a pattern exaggerating *independence*), the child has no grounds for expecting that care will be available when needed. In fact, what is more likely is a consistent pattern of rejection, of being pushed away and left to fend for one's self. The child's response may well be to become compulsively self-reliant and devoid of efforts to form interdependent relationships with others.

Dorothy exhibits at least some of the signs of the anxious resistant attachment pattern. She responds to her aunt's unreliable availability with clinging anxiety. When Toto escapes from Miss Gulch's basket and runs back to a weeping Dorothy, the relieved girl's words—"You came back! I'm so glad!"—can be understood as more than happiness over her dog's return. They represent, too, a symbolic restoration of her relationship with her aunt and uncle. But the fear that evil forces will come again and wrest away Toto once more leave Dorothy with a dilemma. If she chooses the real aunt and uncle and remains, she will lose the symbolic relationship represented by Toto. So Dorothy and Toto flee.

But though Dorothy tries to run away, Professor Marvel's words arrest her. Gazing into his crystal ball, speaking of Aunt Em, he tells Dorothy, "Someone has hurt her. Someone has just about broken her heart." Crestfallen, Dorothy assumes responsibility and at once takes her leave to return home. The rest of her story is one of her efforts to get home. Like so many in this attachment pattern, she can neither truly stay nor leave. She is always looking to find a full sense of home.

Dorothy tries to cling to Aunt Em both in Kansas and in Oz. As we know, after leaving Professor Marvel, she reaches the farm but is not reunited to her aunt and uncle, who have abandoned her to the storm by taking premature cover from the approaching cyclone. (What 'good enough' parent would act like this?!) Caught up in the tornado, Dorothy can only clutch Toto tightly. Then, in Oz, at the very time when she helps Toto escape from the witch's castle—thus symbolically saving her Aunt—Dorothy feels the full force of her separation anxiety. She cries out in despair, "I'm frightened, Auntie Em! I'm frightened!" Alone, bereft even of Toto—the object by which she remains attached to her aunt—Dorothy is overwhelmed by a sense of defeat and collapses. Her insecure attachment at last stands fully revealed.

Impoverished attachments appear to be a vital factor in sexual abuse trauma, too. Perhaps remarkably, sexual abuse in incestuous families may be a way a person tries to protect him- or herself against separation and loss. Although such behavior is wrong, and the abuser knows it is wrong, the need to feel connected may outweigh other considerations. Don't mistake what I am saying: sexual abuse is *always* abuse, and abuse is *always* wrong. But we should try to understand it.

When we hear abusers speak, as they often do, of having themselves been abused, perhaps we are hearing a history across generations of a family where attachment patterns are insecure. When one or more family members suffer from one or the other of the attachment patterns characterized by insecurity a number of predictable consequences may emerge. The anxiety the abuser feels is answered by inappropriate desires to secure a closeness even if by force. Or there may be no obvious force, but a kind of seduction that reflects an impoverished sensibility about the nature of proper attachments, or a diminished self-control of impulses. However we might try to explain it, it is at least plausible to think that insecure attachments may either help set the stage for sexual abuse or once begun act to continue it. Moreover, what a child experiences in the home environment may be continued in the new home he or she establishes as an adult because it is what one knows. It is hard to be better than what we have learned through direct experience.

Fortunately, a history of insecure attachments is not destiny. People with such past attachment patterns can and do learn secure ones. People who have been abused do not inevitably become abusers. And that leads us back to Dorothy and her family in Kansas. Dorothy proves able to forge the kind of secure attachments that serve her well in meeting her needs and those of others. But we might pause to wonder about that most significant figure in Dorothy's life, her beloved aunt. Has Aunt Em experienced in her own youth a secure attachment to her parents? What little we see of her reflects what we might expect from a person who adheres to an anxious avoidant attachment pattern. Emily acts as though she needs no one. Her husband seems more a mere auxiliary to her life than an intimate and equal partner. As she may have known only distance and neglect as a child, so she overlooks Dorothy's needs. Perhaps her own experience was that care meant only a roof over one's head, clothes on one's back, and food on the table. Perhaps her own childhood taught her that she could depend on no one and so she concluded she would look to no one for help. Who can say? The evidence is little, my speculation pronounced—but the guess that Emily, too, is insecurely attached seems a reasonable one. Thus, in this family, a history of insecure attachments may be glimpsed.

Attachment is a powerful motivator. Remember, Bowlby tells us that its very essence is striving to be close to figures we perceive as stronger, more capable than we are. This is why Dorothy calls out to Auntie Em from the witch's castle. What happens, then, when the attachment figure is the source of the danger? Perhaps we must draw the obvious conclusion: the survivor is caught in an impossible dilemma—the very person looked to for protection is the one doing harm. What is a person to do? All too often, what the survivor does is redouble efforts to be close. Though pathological, the response is certainly understandable. The fact that it is so firmly and deeply rooted in human evolutionary biology makes it all the more comprehensible.

Since male perpetrators appear to be more common than female abusers, we might ask whether there may be differences between how men and women experience at least some kinds of insecure attachment. At least one study, conducted by researchers Michael Sperling and William Berman, indicates this may be the case. Writing in a 1991 report in the *Journal of Personality Assessment*, they found in identifying attachment patterns among 130 college freshman an anxious attachment pattern that they named "desperate love." They offer that desperate love is characterized by the fusing of an intense desire for merger with someone else to significant insecurity about the attachment bond. Although this study is limited in nature, it offers an intriguing possibility: desperate love, for men, may be a complex experience that all too often is related to attachment styles where aggressive, hostile, even destructive impulses occur.

I can see the possibility that men who experience insecure attachment may be prone to inappropriate aggression—both toward others and toward their own self. Some researchers suggest it is possible to construct a model correlating trauma, subsequent posttraumatic stress disorder, personality alteration, and sexual deviancy. In short, a chain that takes years to forge its links may start with a boy's insecure attachments in childhood, add trauma such as sexual abuse, produce changes that gradually show in personality, and ultimately lead to the older boy or man becoming an abuser. Though this chain can be broken at any point, it remains one possibility and may explain why some people become abusers. The explanation does not excuse the behavior, but it does highlight how important it is to have secure attachments absent of abuse so that no unhealthy generational chains can be forged.

Attachment patterns and behaviors can be related to every aspect of abuse trauma. Not only the victim, but the perpetrator too may be enmeshed in an impoverished attachment history. Of course, not every insecure attachment inevitably leads to pronounced abuse. But every insecure attachment does come with a price. And that brings us back to Dorothy.

Back in chapter 3, I characterized Dorothy as a nicely balanced person and someone who was quite resilient. Here I have said she exhibits signs of an insecure attachment to her aunt and uncle. Are these incompatible realities? We might as well ask, is Dorothy a different person in Oz than she is in Kansas? I think not. Dorothy grows in Oz. In fact, I say she needs Oz to become the person she wants to be in Kansas. Her journey along the yellow brick road can be seen as one of reworking a whole pattern of relatedness. Dorothy forms new, more reliable and helpful attachments, especially with the Scarecrow. That is why she can whisper to him, "I think I'll miss you most of all." But if this is true, we might wonder why she would choose to return to Kansas and a less supportive framework of relationships.

Why indeed? The answer lies in the great lesson Dorothy learns, a lesson we encountered first back in chapter 1. Dorothy learns that the ability to be where she wants to be is within her. To put this into attachment language, Dorothy learns how to be her own 'secure base' (John Bowlby's preferred metaphor). She finds the ability to rely on herself for her own emotional needs without having to distance herself from others (which is the anxious avoidant pattern). When we make our own self our secure base, we become free to relate to others in a new and unrestrained manner. Unless we can see this in Dorothy, her last words, and the final ones in the film—"There's no place like home!"—will make little sense to us. Dorothy's home hasn't changed; she has. She has become her own home, a place of warmth and safety.

Separations Good and Bad

It may be debatable whether Dorothy's temporary separation from Aunt Em and Uncle Henry is intentional or not. But inasmuch as it leads to the beginning of Dorothy's ability to make herself her own secure base, the separation is a good thing. Of course, that makes it no less unnerving, especially at the start. However, with the help of a new support system, Dorothy in Oz begins to develop more autonomy and grows increasingly into a person in her own right. The secret of a successful separation lies in whether it accomplishes growth, particularly in the direction of making one's self a secure base.

The issue of intentional separation from an abusive family of origin is frequently a critical one in recovery from sexual abuse. Like every other decision on the road of recovery, this one may be accompanied by fear and trembling.

There are gains and costs in any decision. There are also no guarantees that whatever decision is made will produce the hoped for consequences. Leaving even an abusive family is not an easy matter.

I offer again the value metaphor has here. In contemplating such a separation it may be a valuable exercise to seek out stories like Dorothy's. There may be wisdom in identifying with someone else's leaving experience before attempting one's own.

Patterns

Frequently in this chapter I have referred to *patterns of relatedness*. I mean by this exactly what the words seem to suggest: the different styles and mosaics of interacting with others. Try as we might, we all know deep inside that we cannot be without relationships. Ultimate reality *is* relationships. It is Dorothy's relationships in Oz that make it at least as real as Kansas—and for many of us a preferable place to live.

Yet reality is very differently perceived by various people. There seem both to be distinctive patterns broad enough to characterize large groups of people and yet every relationship seems to be unique. Any given relationship may be vastly differently perceived by the parties involved in it, let alone as seen by others around it. It simply is impossible here to attempt any kind of profound or comprehensive treatment of this subject. Instead, I wish to address a few remarks in keeping with the thrust of the recovery process, namely, that patterns of relatedness can change—and may need to if we are to become healthy.

Let us return to the truism: no one is an island—we all need relationships. This is as true for Dorothy while in Oz as it was when she was in Kansas. But our need for relationships does not in itself determine what we will get anymore than being hungry ensures we'll get good food rather than junk food. Erich Fromm tells us that our human need for relatedness might be answered by love and kindness—or it might elicit any number of undesirable answers, such as dependence, sadism, or some other destructive response. The survivor of sexual abuse is often all too well acquainted with these latter answers, any of which may, quite ironically, be presented as manifestations of love and kindness.

Bad as such responses to our need are, even worse perhaps is how we internalize the message that we are only getting what we deserve. Somehow the answer to our need raises in us questions about our own worth. If someone responds to our desire for relationship with aggression, is it because we have somehow signaled that is what we want, or deserve? Amazingly, while we are quick to remind other survivors that nothing they did warranted what they got, we easily assume that we ourselves got exactly what we deserved! Often, it is only though recognizing or acquiring other, healthier relational responses that we finally convince ourselves that our need could never warrant another's inappropriate response.

We have a model in the girl from Kansas. Dorothy needed the experience of new patterns of relatedness in Oz, just as we may. What does it mean, though, to have healthy, secure, loving and kind relationships? From birth to the grave, we all need to feel safe. When close to someone safe we are able to explore our environment as well as ourselves and others. This permits mature love to take place, with its honesty, intimacy, and give-and-take. Our need for relatedness is met when others act responsibly—or as Fromm put it, act as those able to respond to us because they see and accept us as we are. This kind of answer from another trusts us. Our perceptions are validated, our values respected, our desires acknowledged, even if only imperfectly met.

Is Dorothy's story so different from our own? Back in Kansas, Dorothy's perceptions were not trusted or validated. In Oz, her perceptions are not merely trusted and validated, but greatly treasured. Scarecrow's self-esteem soars when Dorothy perceives what a success he would be in Kansas. Lion becomes the brave king of the forest that Dorothy can envision him being. An entire magical kingdom is changed because folks in Oz can and do believe in a little girl from Kansas.

Back in Kansas, Dorothy can only get attention by being in trouble. In Oz, she has trouble aplenty, but what gets all the attention is how she resolves the problems, not how she causes them. This is quite a new experience for her—and a healthy one. The Munchkins honor her as a solution, as do the citizens of the wicked witch of the West's domain. Throughout Oz, and nowhere more than in the Emerald City, Dorothy is praised and cheered. And just as Oz is changed by her presence, so she is changed by Oz.

What is the essence of this wondrous transformation that happens to both Dorothy and Oz? I believe I can borrow a term from Erik Erikson to make sense of the changes: *mutuality*. A relationship of mutuality, Erikson detailed in his book *Insight and Responsibility*, is one in which the partners depend on each other for the development of their respective strengths. In Oz, being a young girl is not a liability. Oz accepts Dorothy on her own merits. Likewise, Dorothy does not set out with a political agenda to reform Oz. In accepting Oz, with all its vibrant, colorful oddities and distinctive ways of being, Dorothy enters into partnership with it. Oz and Dorothy liberate in each other the latent strengths they both possess.

Now I recognize the possibility of identifying any number of other possible factors in changing a personal pattern of relatedness into something healthier. But mutuality is not a bad candidate under any circumstances and it seems particularly appropriate for sexual abuse survivors whose experience has been the very antithesis of mutuality. There is no mutuality in sexual abuse, only selfish exploitation. Neither love nor kindness ever show themselves in one person using another without regard for that other person's growth and well-being. In relationships of mutuality, the parties do not pretend to complete equality (which never exists in any relationship), but they do practice care, responsibility, respect, and a knowing motivated by concern—the very qualities identified by Fromm in his landmark *The Art of Loving* as the basic elements common to all forms of love.

Love, it is said, makes the world go 'round. Does it also send little girls from Kansas to Oz, and back again? Love, as attachment theory regards it, is all about relating to others through certain feelings and behaviors as a way of surviving and, ultimately, thriving in the world. Where there is the absence of thriving, one may question the presence of sufficient love.

Endless numbers of works have been produced about love. Yet in our culture there has been no more dominant source for our understanding of love than the Bible. Some would say that no phrase better captures the most important message of the Good Book than the good news that "God is love." Another metaphor—simple in expression, impossibly rich in detail! To the extent that Christian ideology has pervaded and conquered our culture—Dorothy's Kansas—to that extent this root metaphor controls our understanding and experience of love, especially what we consider divine love.

If we think of metaphor in terms of 'as if' experience, we can translate 'God is love' into God is *as if* God and love named the same thing. But we need help pinning down what love is that can also be what God is. The metaphor that traditionally is employed in our culture to do this task is that God is a strong and caring *father*. To say 'God is love' then is understood as in the context of how a father loves. But such a translation is a deeply disturbing one for many of us.

For those of us abused by a male older than us, stronger than us, and in a position of responsibility over us (whether our literal father or not), the image of a father may not at all suggest 'love.' Is fatherly love—divine love—the exploitation of the young and powerless (the earthly man's action), or just silent neglect while such goes on (the divine figure's inaction)? As pastoral counselor James Leehan acutely points out in his book *Pastoral Care for Survivors of Family Abuse*, when survivors are encouraged to reach out to a divine father the image can raise problems. If the experience of a parent, especially their own father, has not been positive, and they are not exhorted to relate to God as to a father, then exactly what kind of figure are they relating to? If God, as 'Father,' cares so much for them, where was he while the abuse was going on? As Leehan observes, it does not really matter what the gender of the abuser is, because in either case the survivor cannot understand the concept of a parental figure who cares for and protects them.

Dorothy's experience mirrors that of many abuse survivors at least in respect of finding no rescue in the salvation figures of God the Father and Jesus the Divine Son. Oz knows no such personages. In Oz, rescue comes by looking within to one's own power and finding it liberated in supportive networks of relationships whose themes are acceptance, not judgment, and support of the person rather than replacement by someone else. For some abuse survivors, the idea that God loves by making his own 'beloved' Son die (and that horribly) sounds uncomfortably like the horror of their own experience.

To even its champions, the divine love, no less than any other love, is filled with mystery and seemingly contradictory opposites. In some of his late thoughts in his autobiography *Memories, Dreams, Reflections*, C. G. Jung extolled this idea. He reflected that both in his medical experience and in his personal life he repeatedly encountered the mystery of love without ever being able to explain what it is. Love, concluded Jung, escapes rational comprehension. We may talk about it, but we can never capture the whole of it no matter how many fine words we use. For Jung, the matter is captured by the metaphor that for a human being love is light *and* darkness, whose end cannot be seen.

Unfortunately for abuse survivors, too much of the dark side and too little of the light already has been seen. It can be no surprise to find abuse survivors confused and uncertain about what love is when the messages they have received have been contradictory at best and horrible lies at worst. The transformation of relatedness that assists the change from surviving to thriving lies in a mutuality of love where honesty replaces deceit, consistency replaces capriciousness, and balance replaces imbalance.

Dorothy experiences affection in both Kansas and Oz, but it is safe to claim that it is only in Oz that she realizes the dimensions of a love she craves in Kansas. The difference is rooted in the mutuality she finds in Oz that has been absent in Kansas. In Oz the disparity between her power and those she relates to is either vastly diminished, or imbalanced in her favor. In other words, in Kansas she is a powerless little girl to everyone. In Oz, Dorothy is at least an equal and generally is seen as possessing more power than those around her. This dramatic reversal disconcerts Dorothy in Munchkin land. Yet by the time she has reached the Emerald City a second time, she is comfortable enough with her own power to be able to wield it to return her to a place where she can expect to again be relatively devalued. But this time in Kansas, Dorothy has Oz to draw upon. She is no longer the powerless little girl. The love she has participated in has changed her in the direction of healthy growth.

Again, just how does Dorothy attain this remarkable love? Love, muses Erich Fromm in *The Dogma of Christ*, is not an achievement easily attained. Many fail to love, in no small measure because of the insecurity of their attachment patterns. In fact, Fromm speculates, the person who cannot love must resort to another, more desperate way of relating to others. This other way, as Fromm describes it, entails seizing complete power over another person. The aim of such control is to make the other person do, feel, and think whatever the controller wants. In essence, such power aims to transform another *person* into a *thing*, specifically, a *possession*. This is the path of Elvira Gulch in Kansas and the wicked witch of the West in *Oz*. It is the path Dorothy refuses to walk.

Instead, Dorothy and Oz enter into a pact of mutuality that begins with acceptance of the uniqueness of one another's reality. Dorothy does not treat Oz as though it were Kansas and Oz does not treat Dorothy as anything other than a charmed and charming young woman. The Scarecrow grows to love Dorothy because she treats him not as a conglomeration of straw, but as a living being who actually is what he himself only dreams of being. In other words, mutuality means embracing with optimism and trust the hopeful vision another has of his or her own self. Scarecrow becomes himself in the reflection of Dorothy's believing eyes. Dorothy becomes herself arm in arm with a floppy man of straw. Tin Woodsman grows to love Dorothy because she treats him not as a rusted collection of nuts and bolts, a hollow figure of a man, but as a warm and caring soul whose tears are precious. In Dorothy's affectionate pats he feels the patter of his own heart. Mutuality means seeing beyond the veneer to the essence that unites beings. Tin Woodsman and Dorothy are joined by their humanity to celebrate, not decry, their differences. Lion comes to love Dorothy because she confronts him without rejecting him. In so doing she challenges him to become the king of the forest rather than remain the slave of fear. Mutuality means meeting one another at the broken places in order to bind and mend rather than separate and hurt. As Dorothy confronts Lion, so Lion stands beside her to lend her strength in the witch's castle.

The love that mutuality knows is a far distance from the false masks that abuse trauma uses. Sexual abuse distorts love and makes the survivor feel used, loveless, and unworthy. It makes whatever attachment persists an insecure one. Dorothy in Kansas feels the effects of the insecure attachment she has with her aunt and uncle. She knows from the messages that she receives both that she has the power to cause trouble and the inability to solve the problems she causes. Her love is insufficient to save Toto but able to break her Auntie Em's heart. In short, her love is not worthy because on the one hand it is impotent to aid and on the other it has frightening potential to harm.

If ever a girl from Kansas needs the messages of Oz it is Dorothy! In Oz she learns that the love she so wants to give is as earnestly desired. She discovers her giving draws stalwart companions to her side. In sum, in Oz, Dorothy learns that love has its worthiness in seeing and enhancing the worthwhileness of self and others. Who would not choose to be around such love?

The 'S' Word

In human beings, love never seems very far away from sexuality. For better or worse, human beings are sexual beings. Dorothy is not just a person, she is a *girl.* Of course, in neither Kansas nor in Oz is the dreaded 'S' word (sex) ever spoken. But neither Kansas nor Oz are gender free.

Ever notice who wears the proverbial black hats and white hats in Kansas and in Oz? Of those around Dorothy in both realms, the good folks are almost uniformly male and the ambivalent or evil folk are pretty much all female. Count them up: Elvira Gulch, two wicked witches, and—in some respects—Auntie Em wear the black hats. The three farmhands, Scarecrow, Tin Woodsman, Lion, Professor Marvel, and the wizard prove to wear the white hats. Even the male functionaries who obey the wicked witch are really good guys; they did evil only because they were under the power of an evil woman. Glinda stands alone as the only truly good woman, and we are not fully convinced of that until almost the time when Dorothy is ready to leave Oz. It is not a pretty scorecard.

If we think about it for a moment, though, we might see a way that this un-happy picture at least makes sense. Both Kansas and Oz belong to Dorothy's story and what we see reflects her perceptions. Could it be that the women represent what Dorothy fears about her own future? Perhaps she is afraid that only by becoming ugly with abusive power—like Elvira Gulch or the witches of East and West—does a woman have any force in a man's world. She turns from this vision in revulsion. Or will she become like Auntie Em, this woman of shadow as well as of warmth? Glinda remains a wondrous mystery, a creature of beauty who fades in and out with the gentle breeze. She teasingly encourages Dorothy without ever openly manifesting whatever power she has. Her magic is always hidden.

The males, on the other hand, are generally well-meaning and even the bumbling wizard at least has a strong pretense to power and competency. Her true friends are all male, each exhibiting in turn the brains, heart, and courage that Dorothy possesses in herself without real awareness of them. Or does she always have them? Is it perhaps the case that she acquires these qualities in the presence of so much testosterone? Does Oz really mean that women find salvation in becoming like men? (Jesus said: "For every woman who makes herself male will enter the kingdom of heaven."—*Gospel of Thomas,* Logia 114.)

Perhaps I can be excused for detecting some gender confusion in Dorothy's story if I own up to my suspicion that issues with gender identity sometimes may accompany insecure attachments. Dorothy does not seem real secure in her own identity as a girl who will one day soon become a *woman.* She seems mani-festly more comfortably among the men of Kansas and the males of Oz. Tom-boyish in manner, does Dorothy yearn to be a man? Remember, Dorothy was raised in Kansas, and such things are common enough there!

What makes any of us the gender we come to have, to hold, and to act? If we remember our earlier lessons, we may recognize that we each will find our own way. But that way will be guided and steered by powerful forces, such as our sense of our own body and its rhythms, our attractions and desires, our struggles to come to terms with the expectations of others, and certainly with the demands of our culture. Growing up at all is complicated, but growing us *gendered* and *sexual* is especially tricky—and all the more so when sexual abuse is in the picture.

Dorothy no more escapes these influences than any of the rest of us. Yet I must ask: So what if she yearns to be like those who offer her what she needs? I don't think she wants to be a scarecrow, tin woodsman, lion—or male—any more than her friends want to be Dorothy—or female. Rather, all the compan-ions in Oz have the good sense to want to be who they are. If in the end that means a more masculine gender identity for Dorothy than what some in Kansas think appropriate, I submit that is their problem. She does quite nicely in Oz, a land where a tin man can cry freely, and lions and scarecrows trade masculine fearsomeness for feminine sensitivity and in the bargain end up *stronger.*

Abuse survivors, because they have been attacked precisely at their sexual identity, may be troubled with gender confusion, sexual orientation, and a variety of behavioral sexual dysfunctions. None of this is inevitable, but if it does occur it isn't the tragedy that our culture might want to make of it. We are who we are—and important as gender, sexual identity, sexual orientation, and the like may be to us, none matter except how they contribute to our being someone comfortable in our own skin, able and willing to give and receive love. Oz remains far ahead of us in this wisdom.

But we must muse a little longer on a matter important in both Kansas and in Oz. There persists a perplexing relation between gender and power. Though Oz has powerful women, they are styled 'witches' and whether deemed good or evil they rank second to the male Wizard who rules Oz. In Kansas, men hold power, too. They are just as prone to call strong women 'witches,' but less likely to style any of them as good. If a bucket of water is enough to do an Oz witch in, Kansas' witches seem to need a river. It isn't that they are harder to kill; Kansans just engage in overkill as a reflection of their unease.

The culture-bound, entrenched disparity between the power of men and women is a hallmark of our society. Nor is this a modern phenomenon alone. Masculine sexuality has not only been identified for at least the last few thousand years with power, but also with arbitrary power. What's worse is that the arbitrary aggression of masculine power has been justified too often as the natural consequences of normal biology. 'A man just can't help himself.' Even the preeminent philosopher of ancient Greece, Plato, could remark in his little book *Timaeus* that in men their sexual nature proves disobedient and self-willed. He likens male sexuality to a creature deaf to reason that tries to dominate all because of its frenzied lusts. If this is the way a man is in a man's world, what chance does a woman—let alone a girl from Kansas—have?

We might expect that in such a climate sexual abuse would come in the guise of manly gifts of love to a woman who deserves no better anyway. Is it really so surprising women might envy the male member that dispenses power, even if brutally? Should we be shocked if some women despise their own bodies, built to receive such an instrument of power but not built with any comparable tool to wield the same power toward—or against—men? Obviously, our sexuality is a basic expression of our body. Accordingly, the way we feel about the self will work itself out in the body. We cannot escape being sexual, but *how* we are sexual stems from those feelings about ourselves we hold in our body.

I don't know exactly how Dorothy feels about her body. I want to believe she profits from masculine company so as to celebrate her own femininity. But I don't know. What I do know is that—whether it *ought* to be this way or not—Dorothy's significant support comes mostly from men. It is time we look once again at them.

Dorothy's Company

The most notable support in Oz for Dorothy comes from Scarecrow, Tin Woodsman, and Lion. They love her and in the mutuality of her relationships with them they each separately and together grow. If some would choose to emphasize that all three companions are male, I will choose instead to emphasize that while all three are supremely human, none of them is a man! Let them remain what they are: beings of straw, and tin, and kitty fur, who among themselves exhibit the nobility of humanity.

If love is never far from sexuality, it is attachment, not sexuality, which remains its essence. In that realm, the issue is not gender but security. Dorothy grows from the support of her friends not because they are male, but because they provide stable, consistent, helpful attachments. She renders the same to them. Rather than being essentially hierarchical with an imbalance of power and investment—such as typifies Dorothy's relationship with her aunt and uncle--these relationships in Oz are horizontal, between beings who see themselves as roughly equals, or perhaps more to the point, as roughly equal in their lack of power. Dorothy is not alone in seeing herself as relatively powerless; her companions view themselves likewise. In fact, I suspect that the only real equality of power is when no one has any.

Trauma exposes the poverty of power any of us really have. Moreover, as we have seen, two of the horrors of trauma are its isolating consequences and its having to be endured alone. Being abused is like catching an illness—no one wants to get too close, as though it might be infectious. It is Dorothy who rides the tornado, not her friends. It is Scarecrow whose insides are scattered, not Dorothy. But this is only one side of an important equation. What we experience alone can be shared in ways that moderate the pain. Dorothy is strengthened by those who have never experienced a tornado. Scarecrow is put back together by those who are not made of straw.

What happens to Dorothy matters to her companions. It affects them profoundly. In fact, if we hearken back to Scarecrow's own trauma, even in the midst of his own hurt his goal was to be put back together in order to go help Dorothy. Being attached to others means sharing as well as caring. The closer we are to someone, the more that person's pain impacts us. Trauma never touches just the victim, for none of us lives in complete isolation. The community of support, in offering resources for healing, finds resources for its own mending as well. The reaffirmation of healthy attachments in the face of deprivation, horror, loss and pain is a supreme offering of genuine love.

Plato, in a letter to some compatriots, advises one of them of the surpassing worth of good friends. He tells the man, wealthy in horses and other goods, that we will find less power in all those things than he will in finding steadfast friends of good character. I cannot imagine Dorothy arguing.

Chapter 10

WIZARDS & WITCHES

If Ever a Wiz there Was

The tornado whirled her from Kansas brown,
    spinning her along the rainbow's curve,
      dropping her amidst Ozian color.
        No more dust, no more dryness.
        Instead,

        dead,
a witch in black demise ending Munchkin shyness
    in a sparkle of smiling technicolor.
  Then curlicues of yellow brick, swirling, serve
to dance her along to where a wizard can be found.

Oz.
    Dark brooding witches and a preposterous wiz.
Odd, because
    if ever a wiz there was, what Dorothy does
    is wizardry too much for even Oz.
        Killing two witches is serious biz.

And what of dear Glinda, who gets around
    with just the right measure of verve,
      orchestrating the whole maddening color
        scheme like some enchanted Highness?

Ah, now here's a therapist who knows a fine mess!
    Glinda's smiles paint Dorothy's colors
    with just the right blush of steely nerve
    to keep both feet rooted in ruby on the ground.
But Glinda remains Glinda.
        Dorothy is the real Wizard of Oz.

Seeking Magic

What is to be done about Dorothy? As Glinda sings to the Munchkins, "When she fell out of Kansas a miracle occurred." But though the miracle for Oz is the demise of the wicked witch of the East, for a Kansas girl it looks more like a major complication to her simple plans. Being in Oz for Dorothy apparently represents a crimp in her goal to return to Auntie Em, whom she is afraid might be deathly sick with worry over her. Not unexpectedly or unreasonably, Dorothy is openly receptive to help.

What do we do when we discover we are in a strange land and all we want is to get back home? As survivors of trauma, we may find ourselves in young or middle adulthood before waking to the distressing realization that, "this isn't Kansas anymore!" Whether gradually or suddenly, something changes and the world no longer looks the same. Where do we turn for help? In Oz the logical candidates seem to be witches and wizards. In Kansas, the rough equivalent may be one or another of the kinds of counselors who offer their services.

This chapter extends the previous one, which looked at changing relations. Here we shall examine one particular set of relationships: the attachment to a professional helper. No differently than in Oz, some of these helpers are more skilled than others. Unfortunately, some are also unfit to help others. There are good and evil witches and wizards in Kansas, too.

Dorothy is very fortunate to land on a wicked witch and have her first conversation with a good one. Glinda, witch of the North, arrives shortly after Dorothy does and clarifies the situation, which includes a rather nasty surviving sister witch to the one Dorothy's house has done in. We shall look at Dorothy's interactions with the witch of the North and the witch of the West as well as with the wizard. We shall also consider her talk with Professor Marvel back in Kansas. But first, we need to clarify some basic matters.

When the good witch Glinda advises her to go back to Kansas, Dorothy expresses her willingness but adds, "But which is the way back to Kansas? I can't go the way I came!" Abuse survivors long for a sense of home and health as fervently as Dorothy does. But, just like Dorothy, a tornado interferes with our efforts to be there. Also like Dorothy, once a tornado has removed one from Kansas to Oz, or from innocence to terrible knowledge, there is no going back the way one came. Unfortunately, many of us expend a great deal of energy unconsciously attempting to get the abuse right—to somehow reenact the scene of the crime in the futile hope that this time, if only something is done a bit better or a little differently, the whole original trauma will be undone. Perhaps the hardest trauma lesson of all is that abuse is something that can never be done 'right' so as to make future abuse never happen or so as to undo the abuse that has happened or is happening.

Fortunately for Dorothy, she realizes from the start that trying to ride a tornado only guarantees bumps and bruises. If she is to escape Oz, there must be a different route home. That is why she is so receptive to assistance from those in Oz who know things she does not and who might help her learn what she needs to know. Being a magical realm, it is by way of magic that Dorothy can eventually realize her hope. Of course, much of the real magic of Dorothy's adventure resides in her finally understanding that she has within herself all the power she needs to make her wishes come true. Ironically, seeking help from those who know what she does not means her coming to know the really meaningful things about herself that *only* she can know! But coming to know this, to *really* know this, is easier said than done.

Already by the time of Plato, more than two millennia ago, it was an old saying that only a person sound of mind can truly know her or his own self. Whatever promotes our own rationality will improve our reasoning, and lead us to more accurate knowledge and judgments about who we are. It is the process of coming to know herself that occupies Dorothy in Oz. In doing that she also comes to know a community of like-minded and like-acting persons that she belongs among. She not merely exercises a soundness of mind, she acquires it through walking the yellow brick road. And she does it among friends.

We abuse survivors are often quite concerned with our soundness of mind. A great much of the value in connecting with 'one's own'—fellow survivors—comes in the recognition that we are not crazy, but quite normal for anyone who has been subjected to crazy events in what may often be a chaotic environment. The result of being so connected is a kind of settledness that lends stability, a growing calmness, and a better sense of respect for our own remarkable soundness in persevering through the insanity of those who have afflicted the abuse. Our road, too, has fellow travelers.

Dorothy must experience the yellow brick road before she can return to Kansas. She needs the lessons it provides. Of course, when she stands in Munchkin land, she isn't thinking about the road, just the destination. It's not the process of traveling that attracts her but the vision of being there. She wants to be back in Kansas as quickly as she can.

I would mislead if I suggested anything other than that virtually everyone who comes for help in recovering from abuse trauma comes hoping for a dramatic and sudden change. We, too, just want to get there. Even after Dorothy learns Glinda cannot send her back, but that she must journey to petition the wizard, she retains a naive optimism that just asking for help from someone more powerful is all that she needs to find her wish granted. We might call this the hope for therapy by a magic wand: one wave and everything is okay. Yet even in Oz the potent magic of ruby slippers requires a fair amount of walking in them.

So what have we in all of this? First, a strange, unfamiliar, and undesired situation presents itself. No matter Oz's charms, Dorothy wants to be in Kansas. Second, a logical awareness dawns that getting where one wants to be may require skilled help. Dorothy turns to Glinda, who refers her to the Wizard of Oz. Third, Dorothy learns the benefit of connecting with others like one's self. Dorothy not merely seeks individual help, she joins with a company of fellow seekers. This band strengthens all its members. Finally, the delusion that help might come with the wave of a wand and produce instant results is undone.

This delusion must be faced and dispelled before real magic can happen.

Be sure of this: there *is* real magic. Be equally sure of this: magic is rarely a sudden thing, a spell easily tossed out in a word or a simple gesture. The more powerful the magic invoked, the greater the labor in producing it. Nor is magic something safe. Powerful magic is always dangerous, precisely because it *does* change things.

Safety and Change

It may seem safer to simply stay where one is than to risk messing with anything that can make for real change. How different Dorothy's story would have been had she not run away from home, or had she decided to stay in Munchkin land! Certainly any number of abuse survivors hold back from seeking help because at some level we (rightly) fear the very change we crave. Change is fearful, and anyone who says otherwise is a liar or a fool. Change means risk, unpredictability, and the possibility of disaster. The familiar, however rotten, is at least well known.

However, the safety of the familiar is a fearful prospect, too. Such safety can mean the stunting of one's potential, a resignation to an unhappy, unhealthy self and environment, a failure to ever experience the richness of development. Had Dorothy stayed in Oz she could never have become the person she wanted to be in Kansas. Anyone who does not fear the safety of the familiar is as foolish as the person who does not fear change. Neither safety nor change should be either undervalued or taken for granted.

Change for the simple sake of change is perhaps the riskiest business of all. But Dorothy seeks change in Oz for a reason. We must do the same. Where we are isn't home. To get where we want to be means we have to get up and walk. In the absence of a road, we have to build one.

If, as I suggested much earlier in this book, life is about growing, then meaningful change is about *growth*. Yet, as we saw in the last chapter, we need the safety of secure attachments in order to grow out into our environments and fully realize ourselves. There is no simple choice between safety and growth; we need both. However, the ultimate purpose of safety *is* growth. "Safety has both anxieties and delights; growth has both anxieties and delights," wrote humanistic psychologist Abraham Maslow, near the end of his life, in his book *Toward a Psychology of Being*. "We grow forward when the delights of growth and anxieties of safety are greater than the anxieties of growth and the delights of safety." Change in the direction of growth is a result of stepping forth from our safety without having to feel more unsafe.

The magic Dorothy really seeks in Oz remains quite unknown to herself. All she wants is to get back home. What she finds are attachments that allow her to become her own secure base. From that base she is able to grow out of Oz and back into Kansas. Is this any different than what we need?

Change is often an odd phenomenon. We may crave it and shrink from it in the same moment. When we intentionally bring it about we often smugly assume the rightness of it. When it happens to us outside our will we may demand of it a justification. Change often prompts the most basic questions human beings ask.

Yet I don't remember ever hearing Dorothy ask the most obvious questions: 'Why? Why me? Why now?' Perhaps it seems entirely logical that we will want to figure out both if we brought about what has happened, and if our actions—whatever they were—were reasonable ones. However, Dorothy, like many abuse survivors, seems not to ask these questions, at least not right away. Instead, she apparently takes it for granted that she is the causal agent at the center of all that is taking place, even when it is things she does not will or want. Likewise, we often assume that somehow we are responsible—for everything that happens!

The intentional changing toward growth that we can term 'recovery' in the context of sexual abuse trauma involves learning to adjust the questions we ask, the direction those are sent, and the way in which we ask them. Recovery may seem like a commitment to remembering what we want to forget, talking about what no one wants to hear, and confessing a truth too many will see as a lie. So? The memories are ours, the words are ours, and the truth is ours. Recovery means reclaiming what belongs to us—memory, voice, and truth. Yet how we go about these things often requires not just asking questions, but reframing our questions in manner and content. We must learn to question ourselves more gently, other people more firmly, and always with a persistence to strip away the masks of deceit to uncover the truth.

Often, we must first learn to ask 'Why? Why me?' before we can feel the force of the evil done to us, and our own inescapable guiltlessness. *No one* merits abuse, *no one* asks for abuse, and *no one* can escape responsibility for reaffirming a survivor's innocence whenever the self-accusing questions surface. We also need to emphasize questions that *can* be answered, like 'How do I become who I want to be?' rather than 'Why did that so-and-so do this to me?' Sometimes we simply have to learn how to ask questions at all.

Dorothy begins knowing how to ask questions, but her questions get better as she goes along. They become more focused and goal-directed, hence more productive. Through even her questions Dorothy begins to practice a healthy assertiveness; just asking a question can be profoundly assertive. Fortunately, in Oz her questions are listened to and often meet with very thoughtful, helpful responses.

The instinct behind Dorothy's—or anyone else's—questions is the search for meaning. Magic presumes that meaning is always present; it merely waits to be revealed. The unveiling of meaning may occur through either spells of making or unbinding. The magic in meaning and the meaning of magic, though, require special attention.

Magic

Incredible as it may seem to those of us who know better, there are those who do not believe in magic! Some protest that unless a thing can be carefully validated by established empirical means, through replicability and by measurement, it isn't real. But for magic to be real in that way I doubt any of us would call it magic. So for such people magic is defined right out of existence.

Magic is bringing forth, by serendipity as well as manipulation, through appeal to universal but invisible principles, what was already there but unseen and unrealized. As homeopathy proclaims, 'like attracts like,' and magic is able to make the invisible visible because it draws upon principles that ordinarily go unviewed, unfelt, unrecognized, and unappreciated. It is less important how magic works than it is that magic does work. Help is where one finds it.

But this is the language of Oz and I forget that we reside in Kansas. Allow me, then, to put the matter in more mundane terms. Magic is how a person grows into her- or himself, regardless of how—or even whether—we understand it, assist it, or get in its way. Magic is what psychotherapy is about when it genuinely supports a person in the process of becoming his or her own unique self. We can analyze it, run correlational studies about it, develop metapsychological theories to explain it, or simply celebrate it, but it continues to happen whether or not we do any of these things. It's magic.

Magic is real. It may be insubstantial as far as Kansas is concerned, but that does not make it unreal. After all, exactly what reality do we fully grasp? We cannot even completely know ourselves—and that preoccupies much of our time for some of us! So what if we cannot fully grasp magic, if it feels somewhat fantastic? The closest we come to feeling comfortable with magic in Kansas is by and in metaphor, and we see how powerful those are.

Metaphors are everywhere. Philosopher Mark Johnson in his book *The Body in the Mind* argues that increasing evidence reveals metaphor as a pervasive, irreducible, and imaginative structure of human understanding, one that influences the nature of meaning even as it constrains our rational inferences. No wonder magic, meaning, and metaphor present such a solid pyramid! All three are made of the same stuff of life. By magic the invisible becomes tangible, by metaphor fiction becomes fact, and by meaning we find our way to live and grow.

I remember that in this book's introduction we dipped into the idea of metaphor for a while, but it does not seem inappropriate to examine it again now as we consider the mystery of encounters with witches, wizards, and psychotherapists. For some reason, people delight and depend on understanding fact through fiction. Novels tell us the truth about ourselves better than do newspapers. Metaphors, those *as if* comparisons, allow us to see a matter not merely from the side where we are standing but imaginatively from other sides—temporal, physical, and psychological—as well.

Allow me here to simply state five basic propositions about metaphor. First, *the truth of a metaphor is justified by its service to experience.* Dorothy's story is true for me because it works in my experience so as to help me realize truths necessary to my own growing. Whether working with witches in Oz or therapists in Kansas, a good metaphor is simply a useful one. Any metaphor that draws the participant into an experience that brings about a change toward growth is a meaningful one—and magic.

Second, *the teleological intention of metaphor is the experience of growth.* In other words, a useful metaphor is the only genuine kind. Let me explain this word 'teleological.' The term has a rich philosophical history and refers to ends, final causes, purposes, and designs. Metaphors aim at something, and that something is an experience wherein the participant is changed so that growth is the result. The metaphor anticipates actually bringing about this change; it causes it. Metaphors carry purpose within them, and serve design. These features join metaphor to magic and to meaning.

Third, *metaphoric intentionality preserves metaphoric integrity.* This is my shorthand way of saying that because metaphors exist to serve a purpose and fit a larger design, the experience they invite us to participate in is kept from being so purely individual and subjective that it is nothing more than psychosis. It would be very wrong to confuse metaphoric experience with psychosis, where reality testing is severely deficient and delusion is confused for reality. Metaphor relates fiction *as if* it were fact, while never forgetting that it is a comparison and not an equation. Psychosis regards fiction *as* fact, failing to see the comparison because the fiction has so overlaid fact that only the fiction matters—and it is viewed as fact. The integrity of a metaphor rests in its preserving reality testing. In fact, metaphor's growth-producing experiences strengthen reality testing.

Fourth, *metaphors are not language products but language portals into a process of experience.* They are not ends in themselves (products), but means (portals) to something greater. They allow us special entry into experiences, whether past, present or future. Since trauma is rooted most often in the past, the ability of metaphor to move into the past is highly valued. When a person finds his or her verbal abilities inadequate to express the past, or suspects that some memories are blocked, metaphor can join disparate elements inside the person to form a whole strong enough to emerge into consciousness (the magic of making). Or it may liberate repressed forces by breaking the barriers that hold them in (the magic of unbinding). The body itself holds metaphors to aid recovery. An abuse survivor's symptoms are metaphors for stored trauma.

The metaphoric experience also may be verbal or nonverbal in character. Even where a therapist employs a verbal metaphor, the client may experience a nonverbal metaphoric experience—magic. This is in keeping with what Paul Ricoeur, world renowned philosopher of language and hermeneutics, reminds us, namely, that metaphorical meaning compels us to explore the borderline between the verbal and the nonverbal. Metaphors reside in both realms simultaneously, just as they inhabit the domains of cognition and affect alike. The relevant domains may be mixed: through metaphor the nonverbal events of the past, from the preverbal period of a person's life, may allow a transformative adult experience, integrating feeling and thinking components that previously were maintained in separate memory storage.

Fifth, *the transformative potential of any metaphor resides in the biological changes they produce.* For better or worse, as we have already seen in earlier chapters, our bodies are not adept at distinguishing fact from fiction. A charging tiger on a wide movie screen can get our adrenaline pumping as effectively as if we were in the jungle. Our bodies speak through changes—in how we sense, feel, behave. But these changes are purposeful in that they reflect both our needs and how they are being met, or not met. Every body change is a part of a body language we can say is metaphorical in its own right. Perhaps our human affinity for metaphor resides in the resonance our bodies have for metaphoric experience.

Where the Rubber Meets the Road: Theory and Practice

Theory is nice, but Dorothy still has to walk the yellow brick road. No matter what we think we know about metaphors, it is the magic in their use that draws our attention to them. Though metaphors surround us, it is in complex constructions such as Dorothy's story that we most often find ourselves aware of them. We tend to be so linear in our processing of the world that stories particularly appeal to us. A story has a beginning, middle, and end. Its protagonist and antagonist engage in dramatic conflict. Themes drive a purpose; the whole reflects a design. Layer upon layer of meaning adheres to even simple stories such as we meet in a parable. In a story as large and rich as Dorothy's we find metaphors to fill a book.

These days more and more therapists are contending that storytelling is an effective way for mental health helpers to deal with sexual abuse. Through stories can be communicated symbolism, metaphor, and suggestions—all with the intervening safety of emotional distance providing the cushion for handling the trauma of abuse. The stories don't even have to be generated from our own experience; they only have to resonate with our experience. For example, a fairy tale, myth, or legend may speak to us because it echoes events, characters, or themes we find in our own life. Talking about that story may help us connect to and better understand our own story. Once again, the use of metaphor grants a distance and safety that makes the otherwise intolerable possible to be looked at and handled. As we have seen before, the magic of *as if* tricks the unconscious into dropping its guard under the implied safety of a fiction, while the body responds to the metaphor as fact because it cannot readily distinguish the difference between fact and fiction.

Metaphors, then, are a powerful tool for therapists. Metaphors can grant safety while also lending an ability to manage the otherwise unmanageable. Because we who have survived trauma want to change in the direction of growth, metaphors are a natural vehicle to which we readily respond. Survivors have *survived*—and now we look for vehicles to convey what that means. Indeed, our resilience and resolve are apparent in our creativity, which draws upon all manner of metaphoric manifestations to cope. From the moment trauma begins until we emerge past surviving to thriving, we who have experienced abuse can and often do display great strength.

Dorothy's Encounters with Experts

As usual, when drawn to theory I become overly linear and much too preachy. I think it time to rejoin Dorothy. Her encounters with Professor Marvel, Glinda, the wicked witch of the West, and the Wizard of Oz provide four different models of what may transpire when a person seeks help. None of these four encounters are unmixed; I have yet to meet a counselor-client relationship that was unambiguously good. But each has its lessons we may profit from.

Professor Marvel

The first person she meets who might seem to Dorothy like a skilled helper is Professor Marvel. When she walks into his camp he at once greets her with a very natural query: "And who might you be?" But poor Dorothy has no opportunity to reply, for he at once adds, "Oh no, no—don't tell me!" He then proceeds to guess until he hits upon the rather obvious conclusion that she is running away. When Dorothy commends him on his guess, he quickly assures her, "Professor Marvel never guesses—he knows."

This is a less than ideal way to begin a therapeutic relationship. It is intended to reinforce the distance between the one who seeks help and the one who offers it. By emphasizing the supreme knowledge of the helper, the one seeking help is put firmly into a completely dependent and passive role. The last thing abuse survivors need is to be relegated to a passive, dependent role in therapy. By presenting himself as the all-knowing, Professor Marvel denies Dorothy the chance to know in her own right or contribute anything worthwhile to the encounter.

The professor's next question is, "Why are you running away?" But Dorothy barely opens her mouth before he adds, "No, no—don't tell me." He then throws together a sequence of plausible, if generic, reasons anyone might run away from home, such as, 'They don't understand you at home . . . they don't appreciate you . . .' etc. This is doing therapy by the numbers. Any lazy counselor can guess—and be right more often than not—that the person before him or her is depressed, anxious, and feeling isolated. But there is a profound difference between the helper reciting a litany before we have had a chance to even open our mouth and we actually being permitted to tell our stories. At the very least, it is disrespectful to assume and to guess about someone rather than let that person speak for her- or himself.

Poor Dorothy, though, falls right into her assigned role. She is amazed at the Professor's insight. "Why, it's just like you could read what's inside me!" she exclaims. Of course, this only reinforces the professor's behavior. He leads her inside his tent where he can consult his crystal ball. Then follows his search through Dorothy's basket (while her eyes are shut tightly as she attunes herself to the infinite), where he finds the picture of Aunt Em. Using this photo he cautiously builds in Dorothy's imagination his ability to really see into this ball what is happening elsewhere. In her credulity, Dorothy is susceptible to believing him when the professor says he sees Aunt Em clutching her chest and falling.

Now the professor means well, as evidenced by his journeying to the farm to see if Dorothy has returned there safely. His intent is to persuade Dorothy to return home and he succeeds in making her believe it is her own idea to do so. Many therapists are seduced by the belief that they know better than their clients where the client needs to be and how best to get there. As a matter of fact, the therapist is often quite correct in both assumptions. But no one has the right to trick or deceive others into making good choices for themselves. I'm sure the professor justifies his means by the end he seeks, believing that as an adult he knows better than a young girl what she needs. Evidently the good professor is unconcerned whether his beliefs correspond to facts—an affliction also found among some Kansan helpers. The professor cannot know what is best for someone he has not even taken the time to adequately listen to.

What Professor Marvel accomplishes is a mixed result. On the one hand, Dorothy decides to hurry home. This is not an unreasonable goal a helper might pursue, and in fact seems from other evidence to be what Dorothy really wants to do at any rate. Yet the cost the professor exacts for this result is too high. He creates by his charlatan act great anxiety and guilt in Dorothy. In effect, he re-victimizes her by intuitively playing upon the very forces that wound Dorothy at home. Therapy that gets its results by repeating patterns that led the person to seek help in the first place may produce apparent change, but never leads to growth change.

So Kansas is a dead end. What about Oz?

Glinda

The first person Dorothy speaks to in Oz (besides Toto) is Glinda. We might worry at first that Glinda will be no more help than Professor Marvel, for she begins by asking what might seem an absurd question. Witches, like the rest of us, learn by asking. Glinda's first words to Dorothy come right to the point, "Are you a good witch or a bad witch?" The question seems a strange way to begin a relationship, but if we consider the circumstance perhaps it does not appear so odd after all. Glinda is there on behalf of the Munchkins and this question is what is uppermost in their minds. Yet even with reference to Dorothy, the query is not a bad one.

Good therapists likewise must occasionally come straight at an issue. If a counselor acts like sexual matters or events like sexual abuse are taboo topics, then taboo they become. In Glinda's situation, she acts at the request of the Munchkins, who are themselves too fearful to ask the question of a being powerful enough to have just dropped a house on the wicked witch of the East. Given the tell-tale signs of the scene, Glinda's question is completely appropriate.

I imagine the question Glinda poses to Dorothy reflects roughly as sensitive an issue in Oz as asking about sexual abuse does in Kansas. While Glinda is very direct, a softer approach is often indicated. Broaching a subject may entail showing a willingness to talk about it in general before addressing the specifics of a survivor's life. So providing a basic idea of what abuse involves and what it does may be a gentle way of probing whether it has happened. Respect for the person's experience is shown both by refusing to dodge central and sensitive issues as well as in the gentle, patient way these issues are broached.

Glinda's approach assumes some prior education of Dorothy about witches. This assumption is a dangerous one, though therapists fall prey to unwarranted assumptions as much as anyone else does. The answer Dorothy gives expresses her surprise: "Who, me? I'm not a witch at all. I'm Dorothy Gale from Kansas." Shortly thereafter, Dorothy expresses her belief that "witches are ugly." When Glinda informs her, "I am a witch," a surprised Dorothy can only say, "You are?! I beg your pardon, but I've never heard of a beautiful witch before."

One of the surprising graces of a good therapeutic encounter is the client's willingness to correct the mistakes of the therapist. Glinda errs in assuming Dorothy has a perspective about witches like her own. Dorothy corrects her. As often happens, when Dorothy corrects Glinda she adds what is the truth from her own perspective: 'I'm not a witch, I'm a girl from Kansas.' Actually, it is easy to see that both Dorothy and Glinda are right. In Oz, Dorothy really can be considered a witch. On the other hand, she really is and remains a girl from Kansas. This little dialog between Glinda and Dorothy helps each of them learn important things about the other and to begin to create a jointly shared framework. Productive therapy is made of many small moments of negotiating a mutually created universe for discourse and movement.

Of course, in Dorothy's case the assumption that she is a witch is an obvious one. She clearly is female and has great power. A great many situations are initially more ambiguous. Survivors may feel like they carry a mark of shame on their forehead writ in a large and scarlet letter, yet do their best to keep it hidden (sometimes even from themselves). In truth, it is common enough that anyone who comes for help may test the waters by offering an issue other than the one most important in order to see how it is received. Or they may come, as it were, in disguise. If they present themselves as a fiction, and a helper focuses on that, the fiction may be confirmed in ways that make the person worse off than before. When that happens therapy may feel like one more betrayal.

If this scenario sounds like an invitation for helpers to put on their Sherlock Holmes' cape and play detective, it is not. In fact, in one way or another, whether directly or rather indirectly, every client should be asked about whether they have or are experiencing mistreatment from someone else. Every good helper remains alert to the signs that a mask is hiding a painful truth. So we come back to the example of Glinda, the good witch and the good counselor.

The conversation that Dorothy has with Glinda in Munchkin Land is filled with instructive material. I like the way Glinda tells the truth, as when she frankly acknowledges to Dorothy that the witch of the West is "worse than the other one." I admire her way of standing alongside a scared Kansas girl and rebuking the wicked witch, answering her threats to Dorothy with a cheery, "Oh rubbish! You have no power here!" I applaud her use of good touch, gently hugging Dorothy and offering her the reassuring feel of her presence. Even when she offers advice, it is only to counter the brutal coercion being attempted by the wicked witch, who demands the return of the ruby slippers, which have magically attached themselves to Dorothy's feet. "Keep tight inside them," whispers Glinda. "Their magic must be very powerful or she wouldn't want them so badly."

As Dorothy and Glinda talk, Dorothy's wish to return to Kansas becomes very clear. Glinda recognizes that granting this wish is beyond her magic, but she does know what will help Dorothy. Rather than pretend to an expertise one does not possess, a good therapist refers a client to someone who is better able to provide the requested help. Glinda refers Dorothy to the Wizard of Oz. If she does so knowing that the journey will mean more to Dorothy than the destination, she does not say so. Often, silence is golden because it allows the client to fill in the space with her or his own self-discovered riches.

Naturally, Dorothy wants to know how to get to the wizard. "It's always best to start at the beginning," Glinda tells her. What marvelous wisdom! Simple it may be, but getting where one wants to be always starts with a beginning, a single step. Glinda gives Dorothy only one instruction: "Just follow the yellow brick road."

Glinda involves Dorothy in a process that corresponds with famed psychologist Rollo May's outline of stages in therapy as he offers them in his masterpiece *Love and Will*. The process of helping, he observes, involves bringing together three critical dimensions: wish, will, and decision. Glinda unlocks an as yet unexpressed wish when she tells Dorothy, "The sooner you get out of Oz altogether, the safer you'll sleep, my dear." To this truth, Dorothy at once exclaims, "Oh, I'd give anything to get out of Oz altogether!"

With a wish, which happens at the level of awareness, a person enters into a process of self-discovery. Upon her arrival in Oz, Dorothy at once begins wishing she was back in Kansas. It is a wish that never strays from her awareness for, as she tells Auntie Em when she has reached Kansas again, she was constantly telling those she met in Oz that it was her desire to be home in Kansas. This wish propels her voyage of self-discovery. Similarly, the desire to be whole pulls the abuse survivor toward a vision of what the self can be through heightened awareness of the body and of the legitimacy of one's wishes. Rollo May believes that the growing awareness of one's body, wishes, and desires—all processes he thinks are obviously related to the experiencing of identity— normally elicit a heightened appreciation of one's self as a being as well as a heightened reverence for the very quality of *being*. This certainly seems to be the case with Dorothy, who learns to reverence and celebrate beings of straw, and tin, and kitty fur.

With reference specifically to abuse trauma survivors, it is important not to overlook a point that May mentions in passing, namely that the body is especially important in wishing, as a language of the unconscious. Wishes, he thinks, disclose an underlying intentionality, albeit one expressed in subtle gestures, or ways of talking and walking, or even leaning toward or away from someone. In his view, precisely because we are unconscious to such things we can be sure they are speaking with complete candor and more accurately than mere words could attain. Glinda cannot fail to see the anxiety in Dorothy's tight clutching of Toto and the compulsive stroking of Toto's fur for comfort. Her nonverbal language when she expresses her desire to go home is as forceful and striking as her words.

Wish becomes *will* when awareness grows into self-consciousness. May explains that if we experience the fact that our wishes are not simply blind pushes toward someone or something, but that *we* are the ones pushing, then we translate wish into will. If nothing else, Dorothy's journey through Oz is an adventure into her own self-consciousness and self-realization. Will brings wish to a higher plane of consciousness and represents an advance of intentionality. In a similar manner, we begin with a wish to feel better which moves into a will to heal as an expanding self-consciousness occurs.

Will leads to both decision and responsibility. For May, a decision crafts out of wish and will a pattern of acting and living. Our new way of living is empowered and enriched by our wishes, and asserted by our will. But these acts do not make us narcissistic, because good decisions are responsible ones. Rollo May, no less than Erich Fromm, sees responsibility as being responsive to and responsible for those significant persons important to our realization of our long-term goals. Dorothy must and does decide to walk the yellow brick road. With every step she asserts by her will the legitimacy of her wish. She exercises responsible responsiveness toward her companions and responsive responsibility for them as they stand alongside her in her quest. Likewise, we fulfill our wishes and realize the potential of our wills only as we decide to do what is required to take care of ourselves, including acting responsibly with others as a facet of being responsive to our own selves.

One thing Glinda does well is stay out of Dorothy's way. Glinda's touch is a gentle, supportive one, administered without calling attention to itself and at just the right times. She makes no attempt to walk the yellow brick road for Dorothy. There is some wisdom here for Kansan helpers. Abusers act narcissistically in imposing their own wishes, will and control on those they abuse. To survive, we may adopt a manner of accepting authority and direction compliantly, without objection or question. We may redouble efforts to please in the vain hope that we can somehow get something right that will end the abuse or its aftereffects. So we develop a kind of radar always looking for the signal of what another wants so we can give it to them—no matter what it costs us. Certainly Glinda's respectful, nondirective approach bears fruit with Dorothy, who whether abused or not, definitely is a caregiving personality who shows little inclination to question adult authority.

Another helpful thing Glinda contributes is getting Dorothy together with others. I realize this is not explicitly reckoned anywhere as Glinda's doing, but she seems a subtle enough witch for such a good step to be right in keeping with how she assists Dorothy. In Oz, Dorothy is the proverbial fish out of water. More to the point, it does not take Glinda much interaction with Dorothy to realize that this young woman needs friendly companions. Those who come her way are, each in their own way, seekers like Dorothy. If the support group they form is not united by a single identifiable problem in common, it is characterized by similar symptomatology (self-esteem issues, feelings of inadequacy, attachment needs, etc.) and a joint purpose: to reach the Wizard of Oz. Groups are marvelous for helping us learn we are not as alone as we believe. We may also begin to find that our feelings, thoughts, and behaviors are like those of others who have been through something similar to what we have survived. Whatever the merits of Dorothy's group process in other respects, her company with Scarecrow, Tin Woodsman, and Lion certainly excels in helping Dorothy overcome her feelings of isolation, differentness (everyone seems different in Oz!), and mistrust of her own perceptions.

Being in a group can offer other merits, too. Here we may discover comfort in the genuine meaning of that word—an offering of another's strength. In leaning on others we find ourselves helping to prop them up too. We receive and find to our amazement we have been giving—a boost to self-esteem that is well-earned. Dorothy's self-esteem is enhanced in the realization that she truly helps those who choose to go with her on the yellow brick road. Being with these friends is an empowering experience for Dorothy. But merely being in a group does not ensure these outcomes. They happen when the group becomes a community—in other words, when they unite. In their mutual sharing and assistance, Dorothy's band creates a unique and meaningful community for them all.

As Dorothy proceeds along the way, Glinda keeps a watchful eye over her. A good therapist knows how to keep distance, when to intervene, and how. Glinda counters the wicked witch's move with the poisoned poppies outside the Emerald City. She is there at the journey's end. The rest of the time Glinda accurately perceives she can trust Dorothy's own powers and the aid of her loyal friends. As for her renewal of encounter with Dorothy at the Emerald City, that is a time to which we shall return at chapter's end.

The Wicked Witch of the West

Fifty percent of all therapists—the joke goes—graduated in the bottom half of their class. It's the kind of joke we tell to keep ourselves from crying. The unfortunate fact is that there are incompetent therapists practicing, and even the competent occasionally may dangerously overextend themselves. They may reach a point where others might better serve their clients. Although I hope there are ten thousand Glindas for every wicked witch, the fact is there are some incompetent witches and bumbling wizards out there.

Too many therapists come across to abuse survivors like the wicked witch of the West. Like Professor Marvel and Glinda, the wicked witch's first words come as questions: "Who killed my sister? Who killed the witch of the East? Was it *you*?"

The screeching, attacking tone is terrifying to Dorothy. "No, no! It was an accident! I didn't mean to kill anybody!"

Sometimes the trauma of abuse is discussed as though the therapist is accusing the survivor, who may be all too ready to own the guilt. Questions that attack only invite defenses. Since a person's defenses will show themselves at any rate, in itself this might not seem such a bad thing. But there is a time, a place, and a way for everything. A goal of the therapeutic encounter is enlisting on the side of the seeker, not against him or her.

The witch purposely twists Dorothy's words. "Well, my little pretty," she cackles, "I can cause 'accidents' too!" The threat is hardly veiled. It is followed at once with her demand. "The ruby slippers—what have you done with them? Give them back to me or I'll . . . ." And then Glinda intervenes. But Dorothy is thoroughly overmatched. The wicked witch persists. "Give me back my slippers. I'm the only one who knows how to use them. They're no use to you. Give them back to me. Give them back!"

Of course, Dorothy would comply if she could. In Munchkin Land, Glinda restrains her with a whisper. Later, in the witch's castle, Dorothy learns the horrifying truth that they can only come off if she dies. The wicked witch cares nothing about that. "I'll get you, my pretty! And your little dog, too!" Like any evil therapist, the witch of the West is in this encounter for what her client can give to her, not what help she can render the client. Therapy can always be measured by whether it is the therapist or the client who is the center of attention and the primary receiving object.

The wicked witch is the worst of all kinds of expert 'helpers,' for she is only a giver of advice. Talk is cheap and advice is probably the cheapest talk of all. Sociolinguist Deborah Tannen has spent many years studying how people communicate. She explains that mutual understanding is symmetrical. This matters because symmetry contributes to any sense of community. Just giving advice is asymmetrical. It presents the advice-giver as more rational, knowledgeable, and powerful. But if someone is above us, they can't be next to us, where we need them. So they stay at a distance that limits their helpfulness. The wicked witch has no interest in mutual understanding or building community. She just wants the ruby slippers! She is full of advice for Dorothy—along with threats—and her talk only accomplishes fixing an unalterable gulf between herself and Dorothy.

The Wizard

At last Dorothy and her companions reach the Emerald City. Amid laughter and relief they prepare for the anticipated audience. Then they are left standing outside the great doors of Oz's palace, rejected the chance to present their petitions.

In Dorothy's despair after being informed that the wizard will not hear her, she engages in self-blame to explain her situation. There is no hint that she holds the wizard responsible for failing to give her an audience; she assumes that in some way she deserves the rejection. She is hardly unique in this; whenever any of us experience something powerful and unwanted we anxiously ask what we may have done to warrant it. Dorothy has not anticipated not being able to see the wizard and the sudden disappointment elicits a search to make sense of her situation in light of this new event.

As we know, though, her words strike the sympathetic heart inside and she is granted entrance. There the wizard presents himself with a booming voice: "I am Oz, the great and powerful! Who are you? *Who are you?*" The roar is so terrifying that all of them stand quaking. But it is a measure of the growth she already has gained that Dorothy can reply, "If you please, I am Dorothy, the small and meek."

From there the audience rapidly deteriorates in quality. When Dorothy tries to explain why she and the others have come, Oz booms, "Silence! The great and powerful Oz knows why you have come!" Then, one by one, he humiliates the petitioners, finally winning a rebuke from Dorothy. "You ought to be ashamed of yourself, frightening him like that when he came to you for help!" she cries out when Lion faints. But Oz shouts back. "Silence, whippersnapper!" This is a very dynamic, loud, confrontational encounter. I do not recommend it for anyone, abuse survivors or not, for it seems to me both discourteous and adversarial in nature.

At any rate, it leads to the point of the interview. Oz proclaims, "The beneficent Oz has every intention of granting your requests. But first you must prove yourselves worthy by performing a very small task. Bring me the broomstick of the witch of the West." Hardly 'a small task'! This, too, is therapist—centered therapy. It is one thing to mutually decide upon challenging tasks to help a client grow and quite another to set tasks for the therapist's own satisfaction. This first encounter with the wizard is a great disappointment.

The second encounter with the wizard begins as badly as the first, then changes suddenly when the wizard is revealed for who he really is. Therapy always changes for the better when the therapist quits pretending to be someone else and practices being his or her own person. The Wizard of Oz is a well-meaning bumbler. By his own admission, "I'm a very good man—just a very bad wizard." Actually, though, I give him a mixed review as a therapeutic helper. He is not a total disaster at all, even if his wizardry is much below what Dorothy and her friends have hoped for. But by then the four friends have done so much of their own work that perhaps the wizard might be hard-pressed to go wrong. All they need is a little touch for they have already made the great leaps they required.

Sometimes the drive to recover and the resources a person brings to the therapeutic encounter are enough to realize the aims of therapy even when the therapist is less than proficient in the area. In an arena as demanding as the treatment of trauma, finding competent helpers may prove especially challenging. The work is costly for the therapist as well as the survivor. As we have discussed before, an attachment to someone means exposure to their pain and a sharing of their burdens. Most of us as survivors grasp that—and knowing how awful our burden is do what we can to keep it out of others' hands. In therapy we try to protect our therapist. Good helpers, though, convey to survivors a willingness to share the burden because they have learned how to bear such burdens without being crushed. Still, it *is* a burden and working with survivors is *hard*. That, however, is not our proper concern as survivors. We must try to trust that the helper can do as promised, enduring our pain without being too wounded by it. Even harder, perhaps, we must be okay with the knowledge that the hurt the helper feels is voluntarily assumed, and for our benefit.

Good counselors treasure the concern their clients feel for them. It helps make undertaking the hard journey worthwhile. Yet the journey remains hard, often long and draining. Helpers, no less than survivors, may often feel exhausted. They may be confused by the twists and turns of the road. They may on occasion feel a sudden fright or question their own abilities. At least some of these things seem to fit the man who has been posing as "Oz, the great and powerful."

Perhaps we can hardly fault the wizard for feeling out of his league. He had never been called upon to deal with anyone quite like Dorothy before. On the other hand, many professionals in Kansas frequently are faced with young girls who have just been through a cyclone, or whose lives still reflect the trauma of a long past tornado. Are they any better prepared than the Wizard of Oz? Unfortunately, a number of studies indicate that many professional helpers have had little if any formal training in the evaluation or treatment of survivors of sexual abuse. Too often, as in Oz, helpers in Kansas hide their ignorance behind bluster.

I find the wizard pretends to much more knowledge than he has—a very dangerous trait in anyone. But be that as it may, we can reflect upon his words to each of the supplicants. To Scarecrow he points out that brains are very overrated. Personally, I agree. Especially in working with survivors of trauma, the work proceeds best when it stays in the realm of the body and its feelings rather than continually escaping into the head. Of course, sometimes the thinking is the problem.

The wizard's words to Lion are particularly insightful. "You're the victim of disorganized thinking," he tells him. "You are under the unfortunate delusion that simply because you run away from danger, you have no courage. You confuse courage with wisdom." Whether one agrees or not with the last statement, the wizard clearly has a point about Lion's reasoning processes. Cognitive therapist David Burns in his popular book *Feeling Good. The New Mood Therapy*, tells people, "As a therapist, it is my job to *penetrate* your illusion, to teach you how to *look behind* the mirrors so you can see how you have been fooling yourself." The facts are that Lion's behaviors show him to be a very courageous being, albeit also a very prudent one who refuses to rush in where angels fear to tread. In these remarks, then, the wizard scores some telling points.

To Tin Woodsman the wizard gives words that are as pragmatic as they are cold. "You want a heart," he says with a small frown. "You don't know how lucky you are not to have one. Hearts will never be practical until they can be made unbreakable." Naturally this does not dissuade Tin Woodsman. However, he realizes what the wizard meant only a short time later, when Dorothy says goodbye. "Now I know I've got a heart," he says through his tears, "because it's breaking!" Here, too, the wizard has not done poorly.

With Dorothy, though, the best he can offer to her is the promise of a ride home in his air balloon, which he knows not how to control. This proves the last great disappointment for Dorothy, for she misses the ride when she leaves the balloon to fetch Toto. The wizard disappears and with him departs her hope of returning to Kansas. As a wizard, the Wizard of Oz is a bust.

The Ruby Slippers

In the end, Dorothy is left standing in her ruby slippers wondering what to do. When she turns to Scarecrow for his opinion, he sees Glinda arriving and excitedly proclaims that help has come. Dorothy approaches her and asks, "Oh, will you help me? *Can* you help me?"

What a potent query! Dorothy's wish and fear stand naked before Glinda. But asking such questions has great benefit: anytime we can get what is inside out into the open we have a new way of hearing it and seeing it that may lead to change. Still, I doubt Dorothy was expecting the answer she receives. "You don't need to be helped any longer," says Glinda. "You've always had the power to go back to Kansas."

I really like Glinda. For a witch in Oz, she has the potential to make a pretty decent therapist in Kansas. Perhaps one of the qualities that makes an outstanding helper is this ability to recognize and affirm the power in the client. Seeing it—so hard for the survivor!—helps wonderfully the process of empowerment. By this criterion, I evaluate Glinda's performance rather highly.

However, the highest marks have to go to Dorothy. Glinda only tells the truth. Dorothy really doesn't need an expert anymore. She has acquired the competency that was latent within her all along. Snug within her ruby slippers, Dorothy has always had the ability to be where she wanted to be.

The helpers of Oz, both the good and the bad, merely spur Dorothy along a road she still walks herself. And that is as it should be.

Chapter 11

A MAGICAL UNFOLDING

Maranta (Prayer Plant)

Like the prayer plant to the dying sun,
Dorothy folded her arms in rest,
cupping hands to catch falling tears,
petitioning the God of Kansas.

But Oz knew no divinely saving Son,
nor offered her a Virgin Mother's breast,
nor sent a Holy Ghost to banish girlish fears;
the Trinity inhabits barren Kansas.

Dorothy woke instead to find Ozian days bright
with the budding promises of her growing power.
Salvation came in every step along the winding way
of Oz's blossoming yellow brick road.

No sun could shine as fierce as Dorothy's light,
a burning, healing, tear-drenched flower.
It's petaled shadow she swept across the long Oz day
to baptize the red veined stains Maranta showed.

In Oz there be witch's and wizard's sight,
but no wine-bled chalice, no wafered power.
In Oz Maranta relies on herself to stay
firmly rooted in her own soil along her own road.

Like the prayer plant to a heedless sun
unfolds her leaf in knightly crest,
so Dorothy tilted lance at churlish fears
and rescued herself back to Kansas.

"I have a feeling we're not in Kansas anymore."

With those words, Dorothy begins her long journey home. The recovery of her home, her attainment of her own self-realization—these great matters begin with a few small, matter-of-fact words. A simple statement of the obvious unlocks a grand adventure.

Recovery from sexual abuse begins with breaking silence. It is no accident that major world religions emphasize the power of the spoken word. In Christianity, for example, Christ is identified as the 'Word of God,' and the Gospel is 'Good News' conveyed through word-of-mouth from one person to another. Indeed, scientists point to language as the most distinctive feature of being human, and probably the reason our brains are so large. The children's maxim, 'Sticks and stones may break my bones, but words will never hurt me!' is manifestly false. Words can hurt. But words can also heal.

No one can know Dorothy's hopes until she says, "I want to go home!" and no one can understand her loneliness, fear, and isolation without those words being spoken. Talking is the door through which what is inside us can reach the outside. The poison of abuse must be expelled; talking about it is a cleansing process. The old time word for this experience is *catharsis*, a potent term for its connotations of a cleansing that purifies through the emotional release prompted by talking. For some survivors, speaking about their abuse even one time, to someone who really listens, is so profound it accomplishes what they need. But for most of us, we need to talk as often as we can, to as many who will listen, as at much depth as we and they can handle. In short, just like Dorothy, many of us must tell our story again, and again . . . and again.

Breaking silence is easier said by the therapist than done by the client. Quite often, we have incorporated at the deepest level the rule *'Don't talk!'* In some families, this rule governs most of family life. In other cases it is situation-specific: don't talk about *this*. We may never question such a rule, or we may need some distance from our family or the situation before we can.

There are other factors that can make disclosing hard. *Shame* and *guilt* can beset us on either side. We may feel humiliated that we have been abused. We may blame ourselves for it happening. To disclose it is to point a finger at ourselves and to relive the shame. Such feelings provide incentive to stay quiet.

For some of us *fear* keeps us silent. Perhaps we have been threatened with harm to ourselves or loved ones if we talk about what has happened. For others of us the fear is of getting in trouble, or getting our abuser in trouble. For many of us it is fear of not being believed, or of being told it doesn't matter, it's in the past, and we should just get over it.

Imagine for a moment what would happen if Dorothy is not believed by Glinda when she names her home as Kansas, a place no one in Munchkin land has ever heard of before. Yet, though Glinda confesses, "I'm a little muddled," she accepts Dorothy's words at face value, deciding that Kansas must be some far away star. This acceptance by Glinda is the key to her being able to sing of

Dorothy, "When she fell out of Kansas a miracle occurred." Liberated by Glinda's believing her, Dorothy can then speak her hopes and fears.

Not long afterwards, Glinda sets Dorothy's feet to the yellow brick road—and Dorothy begins her journey with singing and dancing. For someone who has just ridden a cyclone, killed a witch, and been threatened by another, the scene seems to constitute a case of massive denial. Get a hold of reality, Dorothy! But who has the better grip, me or this Kansas girl, who for perhaps the first time in her life has been listened to with respect and belief by an adult—and a powerful, female one at that! If we were in her shoes at that moment, might we not dance and sing, too? Dorothy speaks and the dance begins. The initial dance of recovery is a two-step movement: the survivor speaks the truth and the listener hears it with believing acceptance.

"Somewhere, Over the Rainbow" and Other Oz Hits

Dorothy does not choose to be in Oz. Scarecrow does not choose to be on a pole in a field filled with mocking crows. Tin Woodsman does not choose to stand with arms upraised in a frozen stance of futility. Lion does not choose to be a coward. Yet here we have them: all victims of a fate not of their own choosing. I imagine it must be easy to conclude that one is trapped, that life is a grim series of setbacks against which we may at best fight a delaying action until the ultimate blackness captures us. But, doggone it, these folks all *sing!* Put legs beneath them and they *dance!* This remarkable spirit simply begs our celebration—and our attention—for it is the essence of recovery.

But how do they do it? I think they start from where they are at. It may sound trite, but wherever we are, we are at a starting point. We begin by standing our ground, claiming this small patch of internal real estate as our own. Then we expand that ground, a little at a time perhaps, but we do it. More space means more freedom to move. In an important sense, recovery is reclaiming space that belongs to us, which expands our ability to move, which increases our personal freedom. This is what Dorothy, Scarecrow, Tin Woodsman and Lion all accomplish.

But how shall we muster the attention and devotion to bring about such change? Obviously, throughout this book I have been advocating the magic of metaphor. We have walked with Dorothy and her friends across the length of Oz using this marvelous vehicle for change. We have considered it biologically and psychologically, at an individual level and in relationships. Always we have kept tight to the conviction that the ultimate power for change resides within the person, even though none of us lives in isolation and all of us require secure, supportive attachments. But somehow I have carried with me a nagging sense that my use and understanding of metaphor remains too shallow.

Yes, I have struggled with this feeling that something truly important to Dorothy's story has remained missing in my telling. I know now what it is and why I was so long in missing it. I have not talked about the *music.* Dorothy's story in Kansas and Oz is filled with magical, metaphorical melodies that take us over the rainbow. But I have trouble with music. Nothing pierces my own protective shell more sharply or quickly. When I am under stress I avoid music, fearful of its power to undo me. Yet I am aware that it is music and song, poetry in all its resonant splendor, that often first gives voice to we who break our silence. Accordingly, this chapter cannot help but listen to some songs along the way.

A tiny poem, a little song, a hesitant dance—these are the small corners of freedom wherein many abuse survivors first escape the prison of their silence. And such corners, long hid amidst our shadows, exist in each of us. Cast about inside the soul and find the music waiting to be born. Consider the power in putting even a simple refrain to a common ditty like the tune, 'Where Have All the Flowers Gone?' Try these words to that tune:

Where has all my silence gone?
Long time reining!
But now my voice breaks out in song,
Hear me singing!

Start with a word, or start with a tune, but make a sound!

When silence is broken, the morning sun shines. The smallest corner bathed in light extends to suffuse the whole of me. My simple song can radiate its warmth to others. I wonder what tunes Dorothy might have sung, or what little poems she composed. Certainly there is a liberating message buried within her wistful Kansas' singing of 'Over the Rainbow,' and her enthusiastic chanting of 'We're off to see the Wizard!' Yet this exposing of the buried, protected me is a fearful step, one best not taken lightly. In a little poem he entitles, "Dedication," existentialist philosopher Friedrich Nietzsche captures the dilemma of the survivor of abuse trauma:

He who has much to tell, keeps much
Silent and unavowed.
He who with lightning-flash would touch
Must long remain a cloud!

Trauma unbalances our normal equilibrium between silence and speech. Neither wholly sunshine nor rain, neither lightning nor thunder, the survivor settles for being a cloud—and often as nondescript one as possible. The denial of the dark days necessitates hiding within a shroud of gray from the brightness of other, better days. Nature and life are stood on end, becoming as topsy-turvy as any twister between Kansas and Oz. Survivors lose the natural rhythm understood by the wise preacher who proclaimed that "for everything there is a season, and a time for every matter under heaven: . . . a time to keep silence, and a time to speak" (Ecclesiastes 3:1, 7). Survivors are left with only silence.

When we consider the experiences many of us have had, it is easy to see why. Not all poems or songs are bright and cheery:

Speak?
You would have me
leak myself all over you?
I *bleed* inside.

If I open
my mouth I shall wreak
such havoc
one should never see!

It is hard to remember that beauteous creation is born from ugly chaos.

Dorothy in Kansas must herself wonder often enough if her speaking does any good, because others sure aren't listening. So she can respond enthusiastically to Professor Marvel's surmise that, "They don't understand you . . . They don't appreciate you." What a wonderfully enabling experience Oz is in contrast. Here she is listened to and heard. Here her words are believed, her perceptions validated. In Oz, Dorothy can at last truly begin to become the person she wants to be, full and free, her own secure base.

But the journey requires Dorothy to speak, to say aloud some things she must hear herself say. Nowhere is this truer than in the Emerald City the second time. Dorothy must herself speak the lessons she has learned to know them consciously and to realize their unbinding power. Only after she has done so can she use the ruby slippers.

Talking *objectifies* what is inside *us*. It makes it real. Putting horror out into the bright light of day does not unleash it to harm us further but proves rather that its internal biting is far worse than its external barking. Getting it out into the open robs it of its teeth. I know how hard it is to believe my words—I also know how true they are.

We often store years of words. The words yearn to be free, to have their say so that they can give way to things the survivor would rather talk about, like music, and life, and laughter. But the pent up words get in the way of cheerier conversations, and silence reigns. The hidden words, the denied words, the silent words, must be spoken.

Although written in another context, the words of the Psalmist (Psalm 50:21) are fitting for the survivors of abuse trauma to declare:

These things you have done and I have been silent;
you thought that I was one like yourself.
But now I rebuke you,
and lay the charge before you.

Is there a prouder moment in Dorothy's story than when she rebukes Oz, the great and powerful? Can this truly be Dorothy, the humble and meek? Or, to borrow from the wicked witch of the West's consternation, "What a world, what a world! Who would have thought a good little girl like you could destroy my beautiful wickedness?" But Dorothy can and does destroy it. With the cleansing symbol of water she washes away the evil stain. Dorothy can and does rebuke a wizard. With a burst of resolve and angry concern for her friend she steps up to shout at a wizard. There be magic here, methinks! It is the magic of a young girl's voice—and it echoes throughout the land.

There is a pleasing postscript to be told about this business of breaking silence. Self-disclosure liberates us to both find renewed meaning in our life and the pleasurable satisfaction of helping others. *Surviving* means something! Knowing and appreciating we have survived can strengthen us. As we disclose that experience we soon learn we belong to a community of fellow survivors, all of us having decided to bind up our wounds, and each of us eager to help salve the wounds of others. Our strength is magnified in such distinguished company. We draw upon that strength not only for our own benefit, but for others. Few joys exceed that of doing good to others without expectation of reward. Yet we find such giving carries the best reward of all: feeling good about who we are.

I hope by now we are all quite clear that health and happiness most likely come only after rounding curves filled with shadows, uncertainties, and sometimes pain. In all my celebration of the glories of self-disclosure I want to stay honest to the truth we know remains: speaking out may be ultimately good for our health, but in the short-term it can hurt like hell. Sometimes our silence is punctuated with an anguished cry. Like Job of old we may wonder, "Why did I not die at birth, come forth from the womb and expire?" (Job 3:11, RSV).

Whether we ask the question of ourselves or of others, or whether we are asked by someone else, the question calls for respectful honesty. Why *should* one live? Whatever answer we give to ourselves, or offer to another, it will ring empty unless it comes from the very marrow of our being. For myself, I think less in terms of 'I should' than I do in terms of 'I choose to.' I don't have to live. One day I will cease to do so, and if I wish I can bring that day myself, by my own hand. Or I can choose to embrace this most precious and fragile of all graces, see what this particular day will bring my way, and resolve to carve out some space for myself as best I can. I *choose* life. For we survivors, who did *not* choose abuse, who have had so many choices made for us, being able to choose life in the face of so much awfulness is brave, hopeful, creative, and intentional. It can be the ultimate refutation of the abuser's power and hold over us.

But this choice is not a once-and-for-all one. We must be prepared to nurture daily that spark that yearns for growth, that energy that seeks expression, that instinct for life. We have talked of its biological givenness, but we have faced, too, the soul-murdering potential of abuse trauma. We must be honest about healing. Healing words come in all kinds, but they are always honest and they are always life-affirming.

Recovery, I have said, begins with breaking silence. But the breaking silence never stops. Once our mouths are open there is always something worthwhile to say. Ultimately, our words turn from our own experience of abuse to our experience of healing to our encouraging and supporting others to break their own silences. Every survivor who speaks out adds words another survivor might hear that will help break the oppressive silence.

Let your song become an anthem for others.

Hear me, kin among the shadows.
Linked first by chains of loss,
we now are linked by our chorus,
voices joined in saying,
'Here I am!
Here *we* are.'

Our words have chased the shadows,
broken the chains of loss.
Our words witness loud for us,
our song proudly proclaiming,
'Here I am!
Here *we* are.'

I hope Dorothy sings such words the next time she is in Oz among her friends.

"I am Dorothy Gale of Kansas!"

Just who is Dorothy . . . really?

Sometimes I think Dorothy proves the old adage, 'you can take the girl out of the country, but you can't take the country out of the girl.' She remains a girl from Kansas even while taking Oz by storm. On the other hand, who can ignore who she is in Oz? A strong argument can be made that she is the most powerful being the land has ever seen. In a few short days she kills two wicked witches, liberates enslaved peoples, and induces the wizard himself to abdicate. She counts among her friends and supporters the beloved witch of the North, the new regent of Oz, and the top two Lieutenants in the land. This is a not bad total for a young woman whose previous exposure to life seems to have been a few dirt roads in Kansas.

So, really . . . who is this Dorothy?

I have argued that Dorothy changes and grows in Oz. I have contended that she learns life's biggest lesson there: the power to be where one wants to be resides within the self. She becomes her own secure base. She matures from girlhood to young womanhood. Dorothy grows into her self.

To understand this change better, let us reflect on what it means to *be*. On one hand, to be is *to choose*. We can, for example, choose to remain where we are, or we can move. We can belong to our abuse, or belong to ourselves. Making choices leads to another fundamental side of being: to be is *to do*. Our acts don't have to reflect what others have made us do. Now they can reflect *us*, our choices, our being.

Breaking silence paves the way to talking about the self. Who am *I*? Who do I *want* to be? The past has made me what I am in the present, but the future beckons me with untold potentialities. It is up to me to name them. Beyond breaking silence lies the reconstruction of identity. The lost pieces, the broken fragments, the unsatisfactory dark places can now be addressed. What has been done to me can now give way to what I do for myself.

Dorothy arrives in Oz simply a Kansan girl. When she leaves she is still a citizen from Kansas but she is also a woman of Oz. Her personality does not undergo a radical shift. She remains, as she tells the wizard, "Dorothy, the small and meek." But she is only small in stature, not in heart, and her meekness is the meekness of a Moses (Numbers 12:3). She becomes what she does, and what she does changes a magical kingdom forever. Within Dorothy is a potentiality that her wishes, will, and decisions unlock.

Much earlier in this book we considered the biological bases for learning, memory, and personality. Since we become what we experience and show what we are by how we behaviorally respond to our environments, it is inevitable that we should see personality as what we *do* rather than just what we *say* about ourselves. Talk matters, but action backing it up is priceless. Having begun by talking—itself a kind of doing—we must build on our action through other behaviors that help us along our way. If all Dorothy does is talk about going home, and never takes a step on the yellow brick road, she will never get home.

Behavioral changes help us emotionally. An especially important part of personality growth for survivors of trauma is our emotional development. Yet we shy away from it because so much of what we are accustomed to feeling is bad. Many of us learn to cut ourselves off from most feeling, and especially from feeling connected to our abuse experience. Being invited to start feeling again, or expanding our emotional life, can seem risky at best and potentially disastrous.

Yet how can Dorothy get home without risking more hurt and pain? To walk the yellow brick road turns out to require more than feet—it takes heart. Staying in Munchkin land is less anxiety provoking than heading into the unknown. But Dorothy wants to go home! We have seen already that survivors of trauma undergo biological changes that may affect emotional expression, as well as often experience attachments that discourage honest emotionality, or make it unsafe. Dorothy is one of our number in these respects, yet she resolves to *walk*, and that means choosing to *feel*. Recovery from trauma is largely recovery of feeling and the benefits gained from experiencing our own emotions fully. As I noted earlier in the book, health is predicated on *experiencing* our feelings, not necessarily on *expressing* them. As we act in new ways we open ourselves to new feelings, or to old ones renewed in vigor.

A prominent issue in recovery is the place and role of anger. Let us consider it once more (we looked at it first back in chapter 2). Dorothy has a temper even in Kansas, as when she flares in rage at Elvira Gulch—and is sharply rebuked by her Aunt Em. In Oz she learns better how to use her anger, not to express her impotence, but to assert her power. Actually, her circumstances when she becomes angry in the Emerald City are no different than they were on her Kansas farm. In both instances, Dorothy was angry at how another was being treated. But all her outrage in Kansas does is underscore her powerlessness. In Oz, though she objectively has no more ability to make happen what she wants, her anger reinforces her strength. The difference is not the context, but the change that has transpired in Dorothy. In Kansas, every pore of her body speaks a language of despair and defeat. In Oz, in the wizard's audience chamber, Dorothy, 'the humble and meek,' stands forth in graceful courage and unrelenting determination. The fearfulness remains even in Oz, but it is made to stand behind other feelings and acts.

In surviving trauma, we commonly struggle with feelings, especially anger. Nothing may seem so frightening as the rage we feel. But the development of a healthy identity depends on our ability to own and integrate all our feelings. We become what we do, and that includes allowing ourselves to experience our feelings and choose whether and how best to express them. Recovery is deeply emotional work, but it is also the work of gaining a strong and healthy identity. We are what we do . . . and we can choose what we will do.

Identity and the Obstacles of Kansas

We start with speaking and we never stop. But somewhere along the way our words take on a new quality. They begin to reflect a new me. Accustomed to being seen—if at all—as an object, a thing for others to use and humiliate and at last discard, we come to see a . . . *self.* Breaking silence has launched the voyage to acquiring a healthy identity. Bit by bit we are claiming larger and larger areas of personal freedom.

Erich Fromm says bluntly that the central ethical problem for humanity today is the tendency to treat people as *things.* He is right that every such effort injures the person. Abuse treats us as mere things. But so does much else in contemporary life. We would do well to be wary of any and all efforts to reduce our humanity. Our consumerist culture, for example, with all its technological toys threatens to imprison us in things while reducing us to a 'consumer' whose only value is in the size of our purse. Oz is not a place big on technology. A carriage drawn by a horse of a different color in the Emerald City is as sophisticated as Oz gets. The air balloon, recall, comes from outside of Oz. Instead of relying upon and celebrating *things,* Oz celebrates and relies upon *beings.* Oz is a land filled with human longings, aspirations, failings, and successes, though many of its inhabitants are not made of the same skin and bones as Kansas folk.

Evil is clearly characterized in Oz by the way the wicked witch treats others. She enslaves beings, forcing them to do her bidding. She reduces them to the status of objects. The ethical stance of Oz is unequivocal: treating other beings in such a manner is wicked and those who act thusly are truly ugly. In Oz there is none of the haze raised by Kansas dust on this moral issue. In Oz, the abuse of others is wrong, wrong, wrong.

Why cannot Kansas see the matter so clearly? We have institutionalized abuse, made it the stuff of generational cycles, and though we decry it the problem still grows. I suspect the answer lies in roots buried so deep and so long hallowed by praise and reverence that it is unlikely many will even look in the direction I am about to suggest. I believe that the pandemic quality of abuse in Western culture has been nourished and protected by the central metaphor of our last two thousand years, the image of a divine Son dying on a cross by the will of his loving Father.

I am fully aware both that my suggestion will meet with widespread objection and that my perception runs counter to the manner most people choose to regard the Christ story. I am not addressing here either the historicity of what Christianity claims nor the creative way in which the religion has turned scandal into glory: "But we preach Christ crucified, a stumbling block to Jews and folly to Gentiles" (Paul's First Letter to the Corinthians 1:23, RSV). I ask only that for a moment we let the scandal stand so that it can be seen as just that.

I am suggesting that the central image of a 'loving Father' who purposefully sends 'an obedient Son' to humiliation, torture, and an unjust death is one horrifically close to the experience of abuse survivors. We are often encouraged by religious people—including ministers—to "not return evil for evil or reviling for reviling; but on the contrary bless. . . ." We might be told to comfort ourselves with knowing "that it is better to suffer for doing right, if that should be God's will, than for doing wrong" (1 Peter 3:9, 17). Wives are told to "be subject to your husbands" and children to "obey your parents" (Ephesians 5:22, 6:1). I know what it also says about husbands loving their wives and not provoking their children, and how the whole system is built on mutual reverence, respect, and submission one to another. Yet there's the rub: it takes *everyone* cooperating to make the system work and prevent abuse.

But how can a system such as this work when it is founded on the image of a Father making his Son die for crimes he did not commit? This is *love,* sending one's only child to suffer degradation, shame, and abuse? Since when is desertion—"Why have you forsaken me?" (Matthew 27:46)—love? And the abandonment by the parent comes at the very moment of most pressing need for the child. With such an idea of divine love—where torture, humiliation, and murder are presented as its manifestations—how can abuse of our Christian children not be tolerated?

How can the Christian system work when the divine child is expected to be obedient but the divine Father can do pretty much as he pleases? In this metaphor the universe revolves around not only the will of the Father, but his caprice. It seems to some of us to be a very self-indulgent and self-absorbed deity that can demand the destruction of the innocent to satisfy . . . what? A king's petty sense of honor? An overweening self-righteousness that must be appeased no matter what the price in life? Is this picture essentially different from earthly fathers in our own homes who insist on being the all-in-all of their own petty fiefdoms?

Is Jesus the heroic Son of God or the victimized Son of man? Christianity glories in the figure of an innocent person wrongly accused, condemned, and executed, while decrying these same events that daily occur around the globe. Am I missing something in seeing this as a confused and contradictory situation? If the *Son of God* can be treated like this, how much more the mere children of men and women? I am well aware of Jesus' own words on children, but the reality reflects more the treatment he himself receives rather than what he urges. The fact of the matter is, the Christian metaphor reinforces the idea that children exist only for their parents, that they are unimportant and expendable in their own right.

I admit to some impatience with attempts to excuse the strong images we find presented to the world with rationalizations such as a Trinitarian God is not really like a father with his son; that Jesus—being God of God—acts with full foreknowledge, assent, and power. What about, his plea, "My soul is very sorrowful . . . . Father, all things are possible to you; remove this cup from me" (Matthew 26:38-39)? If swallowing up the humanity and mortality of the man Jesus is the price for rescuing the image of the divine Being and plan, then what does that say about the real value of human beings? And if the real humanity of Jesus is affirmed, then we are returned to an innocent person suffering by the will of an omnipotent God. There are no really satisfactory answers provided by a mystery—the Trinity—which centuries of reflection have been unable to present in a comforting, sensible way. We are left with a vision any small child can appreciate: God's Son hanging in misery.

Jesus yields to the will of his Father, but it has at best the ring of resignation to a power that must have its way regardless of the wishes of the powerless. Would Jesus' protest prove any more effective than a child's at ages two, five, ten, thirteen, and fifteen? Could it be the divine Father was just not listening? How can a system of mutual submission work unless everyone involved actually participates in a selfless way, and how likely is that when the root metaphor depicts something different? The so-called Law of Relationship says that the person with the least investment in a relationship has the most power. Where the differences in investment grow, the potential for abusive behavior expands. Thus, at the very point where a disinterested father meets an eager-to-love and please child the likelihood of abuse is the transcendent reality.

There is another dimension that disturbs me about Christianity's root metaphor. It depicts someone dying for someone else. The metaphor denies a fundamental reality of the universe, that being mortal carries with it existential aloneness, the knowledge that we alone inhabit our skin and that no one can take our place in the grave. The idea of a substitutionary death is a fond illusion which, being gratified, encourages people to look for rescue outside themselves at the same time as they demean their own value. Life has value precisely because it is uniquely irreplaceable. Life is not a cheap commodity that can be bought and sold on the cosmic market.

Although I know that Christians claim the cross symbolizes the supreme importance of humanity in the eyes of God, it seems to me to symbolize the replacement of human beings from the place where they rightly belong: pinned snugly to a responsibility for their own actions. If God the loving Father can treat his own Son in such a manner, why cannot earthly fathers treat their earthly sons—and especially daughters—in the same manner? Ultimate responsibility has been removed. Humanity has been replaced by the divine victim. And human beings, made in the image of God, keep acting toward one another like their loving Father in heaven.

Oz, I think, is wise to avoid this scandal.

The ABCs of Boundary Building

Recovery begins with breaking silence, and continues with the reestablishing of a healthy identity. This work centers in the redefining and redrawing of boundaries. In chapter 5, I introduced the idea of boundaries, there with primary reference to the psychobiology of the self. Here I hope to be more practical, considering six simple ideas involved in the building of healthy boundaries. I call them the ABCs of boundary building.

Let us begin with a metaphor. "I think of healthy boundaries," writes Linda Sanford in her book *Strong at the Broken Places*, "as being like green hedges, planted firmly in the ground. They are always growing and perhaps they even bear flowers." It is a tranquil image of something living. Sanford expands her metaphor: "They are airy so that you can see through them but not so tall that you cannot talk to your neighbor over them, shake his hand or look him in the eye. Most important, they are flexible enough that you can part the branches to let your neighbor through without destroying the ability of the hedge to continue to grow and protect you."

Having good boundaries is a matter that requires cooperation. While the impetus for growing belongs to the person, no one is invulnerable to the acts of others. Dorothy has more success with her boundaries in Oz because her attachments there support her growing efforts better than what we see in Kansas. Healthy boundaries are never formed in isolation because boundaries depend on the presence of supportive, respectful others. Without Glinda, Scarecrow, Tin Woodsman, Lion, and Toto, how would Dorothy really know where she leaves off and others begin? Without these others how would she acquire the webbing of support that helps her stand against the wicked witch? Yet the central truth remains that boundaries grow out from the center and depend on the individual for nourishment and strength.

To enhance our boundaries we need both our own commitment to the task and the presence of those we can trust. Survivors of trauma frequently find boundary building a great challenge, not merely because we have had our boundaries violated, but because our trust has been so severely compromised that we are unwilling to let the presence of others be there so that healthy boundaries can be gauged. This reality must be accounted for in a boundary building program.

A is for acknowledging the truth, the pain, the hope, and for asserting one's self in each. Breaking silence begins the establishment of identity by owning that we have been wounded—but survived! However, there can be no identity as a survivor without first accepting that we have been a victim. Dorothy cannot survive Oz without first recognizing she is no longer in Kansas. The full, awful truth must be faced, the pain felt and experienced without reservation, in order for the true brilliance of the hope ahead to be realized. This is not a call for re-victimization; it is a sober acknowledgment that getting better starts with knowing how badly we have been hurt. Like Scarecrow's trauma (considered back in chapter 4), the damage must be accurately assessed. This requires courage, and it is a courage each of us has.

The acknowledging is never *easy*, but it does grow *easier*. The more the silence is broken, the easier the words begin to come. Gradually we awaken to a new assertiveness. Instead of begrudgingly forcing words of truth, suffering, and vision out, we find the way to firmly tell the horror, with honesty and self-respect, owning the pain without being sold out to it, and determinedly facing a future unruled by the trauma. *Autonomy* is a wonderful word, meaning 'self rule,' and self rule means knowing and owning our own feelings, thoughts, and acts. It eventually turns us from 'survivors' into 'thrivers.'

B is for being—simply letting one's self exist—and believing: in your self, in others, in the neutrality of the universe. There is no believing without first learning to simply *be*. Taking time for the self is a luxury that may have seldom if ever occurred to us. I like Dorothy's approach. She keeps her feet to the yellow brick road, but it does not stop her from picking apples along the way, pausing to oil a Tin Woodsman, dancing with a Scarecrow, or doing any number of other things that celebrate simply being who she is. Some might say that being is, in part, reclaiming the child whose childhood was stolen away. I agree. Being a child is not a dismissal of being an adult. It is an integration.

When we can *be*, then we can *believe*. This is our issue of trust. It begins with letting ourselves just be, an act of profound trust for someone who has been trained to be ever vigilant against the onslaught of the world. Once this is mastered, then this tiny fragment of freedom, this scrap of security in the self, can be slowly widened. Trust is never a matter of certainty; it always requires faith. Often this may be helped by the use of transitional objects, like a teddy bear, a kind of alter ego for the self to venture faith in. Then, perhaps, a pet to trust. Later, a person. Not uncommonly, the first person we venture to trust is a therapist. Like Dorothy trusting Glinda in Oz, we may reach out initially from desperation and later learn to reach out in love.

C is for centering inside one's body and for capitalizing on opportunities to grow. Trauma has happened in the body (the self), and boundaries are matters of the body. Healthy boundaries depend on taking care of the body. Dorothy may be in a magical land in Oz, but she still must eat and sleep, and perform the other normal functions of life. After abuse, we often are tempted to put up with our bodies only because we have not found some way to put them away. Healthy boundaries actually are a celebration of the body. Centering in one's body means seeking out feeling, rather than avoiding it. It means indwelling sensation instead of dissociating. It means staying in the present rather than fleeing to past or future. Centering means feeling the aliveness of the body, being in tune with its signals without being overly preoccupied by them. It requires respectful amounts of exercise, rest, and a proper diet.

A body thus well-treated is one ready to recognize and grab the opportunities that come its way. Boundaries are ways we explore our environments as well as safeguard ourselves. Healthy boundaries push out into a benign world just as they retract from an abusive one. Capitalizing on opportunities means allowing our boundaries to be stretched for growth rather than bashed by abuse. It means taking appropriate, calculated risks, and represents perhaps the ultimate mark of how far we have come in recovery.

However, boundary building, though it yields true and sensible control, may seem at first to threaten it.

Although I have discussed the psychobiology of control in my *Biological Foundations for a Psychobiology of Abuse Trauma,* a single remark seems advisable here to remind us that a preoccupation with control is rooted in a biological striving for adaptation. As I wrote there, "In adaptation, organisms seek to adjust to stress by reasserting the control that either has slipped from their hands or threatens to do so." Keeping silence is just one aspect of this desperate clutching at control.

Dorothy asserts a measure of control by single-mindedly walking the yellow brick road. Nothing can deter her. As long as there is road to walk, she has a purpose. The meaning of her actions keeps her feeling a measure of control. Only the wicked witch threatens to undo that control and, for a moment in the witch's castle, this is exactly what seems to have happened.

We can speak imaginatively of Dorothy's defenses being breached by the wicked witch's assault, or we can psychologically assess Dorothy as inadequate to the task of adapting to her environment, but whether we focus on what the witch does or how Dorothy responds the outcome is the same—she is overwhelmed. Bereft of her friends, left without even Toto, and mocked by the wicked witch, Dorothy has no more ways of asserting control. She does what she can—she collapses in sobs. Yet in her defeat, crying is a first positive step.

Think about. *Coping* can mean one of three things: we leave the environment we find stressful, we change that environment, or we change ourselves. Dorothy cannot escape the castle, nor can she change who her captor is. So she adjusts. Her crying is actually the most adaptive thing I can see for her in the moment, even if it arises from despair. Control issues may arise when we try to change our environment where adjustment is the more reasonable course of action. If Dorothy storms the door she only ends up injuring herself and risking her ability to act should the opportunity present itself. I don't see her tears as a complete capitulation to fate, but as an honest appraisal of a reality too big for anything but tears at the moment.

Efforts at control are frequently efforts to make the world conform to what we insist it must be regardless of the facts. Doesn't work well, does it? Yet an alternative remains to resignation. Dorothy's crying is not capitulating to the circumstance but releasing her feelings about it. Effective coping can entail either problem-solving or what we might term 'feeling-solving.' If the facts of our situation are such we can alter them through constructive action, then that is the better course of action. If the situation cannot be changed, we can still solve our feelings about it. The key, of course, is recognizing when the facts are unalterable. Either way, we have a clear way ahead to do something positive and thus assert some degree of control. Dorothy's crying is a positive act of 'feeling-solving.' Seen that way, it makes more sense how she is ready to act when the moment comes to do more than cry.

Abuse survivors often have control problems because our experience has taught us that we cannot change the environment in our favor and adapting to it is painful as well. Forced to often adopt extreme tactics (e.g., dissociation, repression, multiple personality fragmentation) in order to stay alive, we may retain this extreme coping style even where it is no longer required and is counterproductive. Our life-preserving solutions become handicapping problems.

Put another way, sometimes our solutions can become problems. Sometimes a solution works a first time, but fails a second. Sometimes it *seems* to work only to prove later that it has not. Sometimes it plain fails but still seems so promising that it becomes an irresistible temptation. The worst kind of problem, though, is the solution that used to work, but doesn't any longer, yet we persist in using it. We can't let go. We act according to the old saying, 'Better the devil you know, than the devil you don't know.' We hold on to the familiar because we fear the unknown of a different solution will bring worse results.

Re-establishing control means strengthening our boundaries. Working on building better boundaries requires giving up outdated solutions. This is a very difficult thing to ask, and it takes time. Any pattern years in the making is not likely to be days in the breaking. The rigidly held obsession with control must be relaxed enough to permit new ways to be given at least a chance.

It is absurd to think that control can or should become a non-issue for abuse survivors. All of us strive for control; the instinct is a normal and healthy one, within limits. But what may be very useful for us is a very concrete tool that can allow the need for control to both be harnessed and directed in a positive direction. I am speaking about purposeful symbols, rituals and other creative acts, which have the power to direct, contain, and transform much of our feeling about the abuse experience. It is to such creative acts—especially to symbols and rituals—that we must now turn.

Symbols & Rituals

I find myself frequently reminding people who come to me for help that *insight* is only half of what therapy is about—*application* is the necessary second half. Dorothy can hear Glinda tell her the road leads to Oz, she can see the road and she can watch others upon it. But to get to Oz she has to walk the road. Insight is one of those 'necessary, but not sufficient' conditions we encounter in life. It prepares the ground for application. I try to follow a person's insight into her situation with a supportive, "Yes!—and what are you going to do with that?"

I am not as sold on the necessity to relive the trauma as some therapists seem to be. Facing the past does not require retracing every step through it. While it is important for us and for our helpers to validate the reality of the sexual abuse and the power and legitimacy of our feelings about it, the reliving of emotionally traumatic memory and any emotional catharsis accompanying this experience is not, in and of itself, always curative. We are our bodies and our bodies often require very concrete acts and products to fully resolve the held trauma. It is for this reason that symbols embedded in rituals can be of great significance. They put metaphors into concrete shapes and form stories out of actions.

Surely Rollo May is correct in observing in his book *Power and Innocence* that we forget at our peril that human beings are symbol-making creatures. Though many of us may find the symbols in the culture around us arid and dead, I think May is right that we are better mourning their loss than denying their potential to help us. He says rather pointedly that the bankruptcy of our symbols should be seen for what it is—a way station on the path of despair. Personally, I think one of the worst aspects of abuse is the thorough destruction of symbols, implicitly backed by the dominant metaphor of Western culture.

A challenge of recovery is finding a rebirth of symbols, though not necessarily the old symbols that have been distorted or crushed. Every survivor's imagination will be drawn to one or another symbol or set of symbols that offers unique meaning for her or his own experience. For me, the ideas of chivalry, honor, and duty as expressed in the Arthurian legends have been attractive. The ideas are powerfully established by the legend's symbols and metaphors. Obviously, a certain girl from Kansas caught my eye, too.

What matters is that there be symbols for us to fix our eyes upon. Survivors have no national memorial, no wall at which to weep as the names are read. Lacking a wall, we must turn to other, more personal symbols. These may be mental images or solid objects. It matters not, for as I have written elsewhere, "depth of meaning is what gives symbols their vitality."

Symbols increase their strength when embedded in rituals. The added dimension is one of teleology (purpose, design, and cause). Elsewhere I have defined ritual with an emphasis on its communal nature. But the definition I gave it there fits here as well: "A ritual is a formalized act or series of acts. The ritual organizes symbols so that collectively they have a certain direction and end." I believe rituals are very powerful when properly formed and used. In fact, in my book *12 Magic Wands*, rituals occupy a place as one of the dozen wands that a person can employ to liberate transforming magic in their lives. Rituals bind symbols together in action and thereby weave layers of meaning into a whole.

Rituals feel solid because they have a firm form. They are self-consciously imbued with symbolic meaning. Their intentionality is palpable. In appealing to symbols, we can align ourselves with transcendent meaning. In participating in ritual we can put hands and feet to the symbols we cherish. Thus, rituals enhance symbols.

There is a profound difference between rituals and compulsive behaviors. Survivors are commonly all too familiar with obsessions, compulsions, and addictions. A ritual varies from these in not having to be done. It is an intentionally chosen and willed act, one stemming from desire, not need. Ritual may be done once, or repeated, but as often as it is done it must follow from choice rather than compulsion. In fact, sometimes rituals can help put an end to compulsions and mark the death of an addiction.

Rituals often serve best when they are *marker events*. A marker event is a ritual done only once to serve as a signpost in a person's experience of some especially significant event. A funeral is a marker event ritual. Putting on a funeral for something can be as profoundly moving to us as burying a person. Marker events help show us where we have been, how far we have come, and that we need not stay in the past.

Rituals, though communal in nature, need not be overtly so. The solitary individual who enacts a ritual alone may be no less united with others whose experiences support his or her own. Nor do the rituals chosen need to be ones used or known by others. Whether we transform a familiar ritual or invent a new one, our creative act brings order out of chaos and rejoins us to the flow of a purposeful life. Some survivors find delight in making rituals for all the places broken by the experience of abuse, including events like birthdays or holidays. Others of us find it enough to use one or two ritual acts for highly symbolic and powerful matters like burying the abuse or letting go of blame.

The only common element in a useful ritual is the incorporation of symbols and acts the individual finds meaningful. Though recovery can proceed without rituals, it is unlikely to do so without symbols. To use rituals is simply to acknowledge the bodily nature of human experience and to use it for healing.

Meaning

Dorothy accomplishes something truly magical when she finds a way to move between Oz and Kansas that does not require the trauma of a cyclone. *Recovery has happened when the trauma is no longer how a person journeys from one place to another.* Or, if we wish to say it differently, recovery is characterized by making choices not dictated by the experience of abuse.

The trauma never disappears; it happened. But it can be reduced in present experience from the status of an all-consuming monster to a single fact of what life has been in the past. Once it meant everything. Now its meaning has been set into a more comprehensive whole. Viktor Frankl, an existentialist psychotherapist and a survivor of the Nazi death camps, reminds us in his autobiography *Man's Search for Meaning* that while the meaning of life always changes, it never ceases to be. We can and do learn that the meaning of trauma is not the entirety of the meaning of our lives. Given the chance, life can and will go on, growing beyond, around, past and through the trauma.

Dorothy's tornado brings her to Oz. As important a place as it is to her, though, she cannot remain there. She does not want to stay. She remains a citizen of Kansas. But with all her losses, in both Kansas and in Oz, Dorothy is able to keep focused on what she retains. In his tremendous book, *When Bad Things Happen to Good People*, dedicated to the innocent who suffer, Rabbi Harold Kushner impresses me with his recognition of those among us who have "the grace to remember what they have left instead of what they have lost."

Dorothy is certainly to be numbered among the saints.

Chapter 12

BRICK BY BRICK

What are Yellow Brick Roads for?

No one ever *marches* along yellow brick;
   the color is all wrong for marching.
                            But not for singing!
                            Not for dancing!

       Yellow brick roads are meant to swirl
   and twist like melodies.
        Girlish curls are meant to fall in braids
          and jump like monkeys on a string.

And if it ever makes complete sense,
                    why,
        then something is quite wrong
          and this isn't Oz after all.

      But somehow,
         amid or through or because
             of all the skipping
              and singing,
        and whooping and hollering

and even with all the breathless panting

                we surprise ourselves
       by discovering that we've sung
                and danced
               and occasionally stumbled
  our way *home*.

And that is what yellow brick roads are for.

"There's no place like home. . . . There's no place like home. . . . There's no place like home. . . ." Eyes shut tightly, heels clicking together in cadences of three, Dorothy concentrates her powers on going *home*. And she gets there.

We, too, are nearly to the end of our journey together. In following Dorothy around Kansas and Oz, I hope we have found some useful images to guide our mind's eye along our own roads. In this final chapter I wish merely to highlight a few items I think will be of special interest to any fellow traveler. These include looking at the role of obstacles, returning again to our bodies, mourning our inevitable losses, recovering a sense of spirituality, reckoning the cost, and hoping in the future.

We begin with *obstacles*. There are many, but perhaps two pose the greatest challenges at the start. First, we want recovery not to hurt. We know it will, but we shy away from that, deny it, or simply avoid doing anything that brings pain. Second, we want—like preschoolers—to do it 'by myself!' We gut it out as long as we can in splendid isolation—except it doesn't feel all that splendid. These two obstacles are the Scylla and Charybdis that taunt us as we pursue health. The Scylla of recovery is the six-headed beast of pain that yelps at us that more suffering can't possibly be the way to health. The Charybdis of recovery is the swirling whirlpool of isolation that invites us to drown rather than reach out a hand to anyone else. But Dorothy suffers to get home, and she draws comfort from friends who step with her through the pain.

Why does recovery hurt? It is like a broken bone in our leg that has gone untended too long a time. Left to itself it makes what adjustments it can, supporting the leg so that one can walk, albeit with a limp and much discomfort. The doctor says the leg must be rebroken and set anew, so that the mending can be straight and firm. The prospect is unappealing. The pain of the procedure is real. For a while, the leg must feel worse in order to get better.

Therapists are not really perverse when they congratulate clients for feeling miserable. They simply know that feeling worse often precedes feeling better. Recovery is not the pain of unhealed suffering, but the pain of attentive mending. Pain can either sit there to remind us of matters still left undone, or it can serve us to build a better future. The *painful* choice is ours.

The second great obstacle we mentioned is a reluctance to accept help, or the insistence on doing everything by one's self. Put either way, the condition is one of isolation. Alone again. What an empty way to work toward the greatest triumph of one's life. Looked at in that way, it doesn't make much sense, does it? Recovery should be a triumph fleshed out in the midst of cheering supporters.

At the same time, though, we must guard against the seemingly opposite extreme: *dependency*. Actually, it only seems opposite. In reality, dependent people are among the loneliest of all. In dependency, one surrenders personal autonomy and clings to an attachment figure in the expectation that this stronger, more competent other will provide salvation. Instead of trying to do it alone, the dependent person tries to get others to do it all. But the result—isolation—is the same. Having yielded the self to the powers of others, the self is left empty, powerless, and alone. Dependent people are self-defeating because they give up themselves in the hope of rescue by others. What is then left to rescue, save an empty shell? The dependent person reduces her- or himself to the status of an object to be used or discarded by those who have the power.

Let me add a third great obstacle virtually all of us must face down again . . . and again . . . and again. Recovering is like giving birth. It hurts, it requires support, and *it takes time*. Impatience threatens to abort recovery before the miraculous child can come fully to term. Premature babies have decreased chances for survival; refusing to carry recovery to term jeopardizes all of the investment we have made to that point.

Dorothy in Oz does not at first want to *go* home so much as she wants simply to *be* home. Many of us are like that. We know where we want to be and we just want to be there. The steps required to getting there look tedious at best and torturous at worst. However, the first steps are almost inevitably the hardest, for they are like an injured person learning to walk again. Each painful step, though, adds strength. Interestingly, the last step hardly feels like a step at all. It has more the feel of just clicking one's heels three times and wishing, with eyes closed, "There's no place like home." But that is because by the time the last step is taken so many others have already occurred along the yellow brick road that home really is just an eye blink away.

Still, Dorothy may seem a mystery to us. How does a mere stripling of a youth from Kansas manage to survive the cyclone to walk the yellow brick road? Then, how does Dorothy endure the pain, overcome the isolation, and curb her impatience on the journey long enough to succeed? Those who don't know her might imagine she accomplishes these feats with gritted teeth, balled fists, and a stolid, determined march. Hut, hut, hut!

Of course, nothing could be further from the truth. Dorothy sings and dances her way along great stretches, and even where the going is rough, she never loses her ability to give a tearful little smile, or acknowledge that behind every cloud there must be lurking a rainbow. She is no Pollyanna—she is simply resolved to find the lightest streak in any cloth of gray. This transcends the power of positive thinking and moves into the realm of creating one's own reality through persistent good will toward self and others.

In his *Ecce Homo*, Nietzsche writes, "I know of no other means of dealing with great tasks, than as *play*. . . ." Dorothy has mastered this important lesson. Without denying the reality of obstacles, recovery sees in them not an end to progress but a proving of progress made. Some prefer the term 'challenges,' for in recovery every obstacle is like a sentry calling out for a password that only the survivor can find, and then only within the self. It may be a deadly serious game—all the best games are—but it remains a game. Play is the only sure way to win at any game.

Nietzsche says something else in this regard that I find helpful. "Everything decisive comes to life," he proclaims, "in defiance of every obstacle." There is a degree of assertive willfulness that meets pain, isolation, and impatience with a proverbial spit in the eye. Pain is more than endured—it is embraced with an appreciation for our ability to feel and to feel deeply. Isolation is cast aside with a conscious decision to risk as often as it takes to find those who make the risk worthwhile. Impatience is chewed up and swallowed down with a sense of humor and a good-natured resolve to stay with the road to the end. *Recovery takes courage.* I like the word *chutzpah.* Recovery is a defiant act, because it refuses to let the broken places stay broken.

Obstacles are never welcome, but when they come, the most defiant course is to welcome them as challenges that will be met. Healthy surviving never involves wallowing in pain, but it may mean sitting in it for a time. Some things do have to be faced alone, but the courage to grab a hand when really down and out takes the courage of trust when every significant trust has been busted before. Impatience may return to us like a persistent cold, but recovery sees breaks in the process as vacations, not resignations from the work.

Obstacles, too, have their purpose, and it is a significant one. In their own way they are markers of our progress. Pain marks our present, showing us where we are now. Isolation marks our past, showing us as we overcome it how far we have moved from the shame and alienation of the trauma. Impatience marks our future, for it recognizes that there is a goal, a place of rest, an oasis in the desert. We are drawn to look always ahead at the elusive place we want to be. Occasionally, however, we can afford to look back and see how far we have come.

Forgiving the Body

Dorothy never permits the fact that she is a girl from a faraway land discourage her. She may tell the wizard she is "Dorothy, the humble and meek," but that does not mean she is Dorothy, the powerless and defeated. By accepting her self—which means being honest about her body—Dorothy never lets her self get in the way. She refuses to be her own worst enemy.

How remarkable this is! By all rights, a young Kansas girl has no business contending with witches. Let's be real here: young girls just aren't equipped to handle Oz. At least, so must go the conventional wisdom. Girls aren't built like heroes. Their bodies are designed to serve as perfect victims, not as vanquishers of evil witches.

Fortunately, neither Oz nor Dorothy let conventional Kansan logic dictate the course of events. Oz is an improbable land at best—by the standards of Kansas. Cyclones strong enough to throw houses on witches should certainly be strong enough to kill a girl and her dog. Witches evil and powerful enough to make a wizard cower and enslave kingdoms should be more than able enough to burn up Scarecrows, rust tight tin woodsmen, make Lion stew, and utterly destroy any odd girl who wanders along. The apparent truth is that bodies of straw, tin, kitty fur, and young flesh are just commodities to be bought sold, used, and destroyed at the whim of those with the real power.

But Oz proves what real power is. The power recovery cares about is found in the body, which was strong enough to survive in the trauma, strong enough to maintain life after the trauma, is strong enough to seek and gain health now, and is strong enough to take a person where he or she wants to be. The sternest test of faith we have is believing in this strength, trusting it, and disavowing the lies inherent in the trauma.

Abuse says the body betrays us. The truth is that the body kept us alive, preserving a core of integrity against overwhelming forces. Abuse says the body is weak because it could not resist the abuser. The truth is that the body is strong because it kept its tiny corner of freedom against a force that sought complete enslavement. Abuse says the body belongs to the abuser. The truth is the body belongs to the self—is the self—and for so long as the self lives it pushes through the cold, hard ground of abuse's winter to emerge into the spring warmth of self-realized blossoming. Believing the truth sets the self progressively freer.

We have seen in this book what marvelous beings we are. We are a startling oddity among the living creatures that share this world with us. The human capacity to learn and to remember, the profound resiliency of human coping, depend on a lack of biological hardwiring such as found in other animals. Instinctive regulation has, in human beings, taken a decidedly second position in the arsenal of adaptation to the environment. This has been an evolutionary step not without its price. A human being, observes Erich Fromm in *Man for Himself*, is the most helpless of all animals. But, he immediately adds, our weakness is the basis for our strength because it prompts us to develop those specifically human qualities that have helped us survive and even exercise dominion. Where abuse focuses upon the weakness of our biological condition, recovery celebrates the strengths made possible by this same condition.

Nevertheless, my saying these things is not enough to make them felt realities for many of us who have experienced so powerfully the weakness of the body, but not its strength. For many of us the transition from the experience of weakness of trauma to the strength of recovery requires the bridge of self-forgiveness. To heal the body may mean consciously forgiving it. We are weak. We are vulnerable. Our bodies betray us. Can we forgive the body its weakness, vulnerability and betrayals?

We discussed forgiveness in chapter 2, but there our emphasis was on how this relates to others, rather than to the self. Here I wish to encourage consideration of a formal act or ritual of forgiveness of the body. This might mean a solemn baptism or special cleansing, as beneath a waterfall or in a spring of water—the place matters only in its significance for us. Or the ritual might be fire, in walking upon coals, or passing through a circle of fire, or sitting within such a circle on a clear night. The act itself is secondary to the symbolic meaning it has for we who do it. The point is to find a way to mark the forgiving of the body for its weakness in order to clear the way to celebrate the body's *strength*, because despite the vulnerability, weakness and betrayal, our bodies *survived*.

Our thinking about this necessitates our pausing a moment longer to consider other losses that may elicit a mourning response that preempts our ability to celebrate.

Losses

Dorothy wants to get home so badly she can taste it. Yet when the moment arrives, she cannot express her joy until she has passed through a time of grieving her losses. Leaving Oz means leaving a land of beauty and triumph, a place of secure attachments, an enchanted land wherein a girl became a woman. To return to Kansas means mourning the absence of Oz. So Dorothy clings tightly but briefly to each of her friends, sharing with them a moment of tears and farewells.

The losses of Dorothy, though, pale next to the magnitude of those faced by survivors of abuse trauma. So many losses! I know we have talked of these before, but just as the yellow brick road twists and turns and curves back upon itself, so in our recovery we find ourselves repeatedly revisiting certain matters. I remember reading somewhere that a therapist who worked with survivors of abuse trauma estimates it takes some 1500 hours of crying for many to mourn their losses. That is a long time—over six months of crying eight hours a day! No wonder some survivors feel they start crying and it just never seems to stop. But the tears are cleansing the body—the self—and readying a new vessel for the joys ahead. There is no limit as to how much crying is 'okay'—whatever a survivor needs is okay.

Then there are others among us who confess how dry and cold we feel. Our grief is a well so deep that the water within has not been able to come to the surface. We find our inability to cry a frustrating sign of emptiness. More truly, it is an indication of how deeply wounded we have been and how far we have had to bury the hurt and losses. Like a deep, dry well that requires priming, we may need to learn how to mourn for another's losses so that we can liberate the tears our own losses so desperately yearn.

The losses, when left unmourned, complicate the process of bereavement so that by the time recovery begins, which may be years after the abuse has stopped, the grief is so entrenched and blocked that the mourning is an especially difficult process. Patience is well-advised. That patience is easier to achieve if it stems from a well-deserved compassion.

Connecting to someone else's pain may help, but so also might having someone else connect to ours. In sharing our pain, and having it received, bonds are built that strengthen both parties. Helpers, who offer bits of their own persons, who confess how they feel about what they are sharing with survivors, encourage trust. And that makes continuing on easier.

Grieving is painful, yet it is facilitated by the supportive help of others, and although it takes time, it is time well-spent. Here again rituals can be potent aids. Survivors must count their losses before they can truly reckon what they have left and move forward.

Grieving is a process, not a once-and-forever-done deed. Though Dorothy may cry in Oz before she can smile at the prospect of being home, she shall certainly cry in Kansas, too, when she recalls her lost friends. Trauma brings losses that can be integrated, but they remain real losses. Occasionally, here and there along the road, the specter of a remembered loss rises to elicit a moment of sadness or a tear or two. These are not moments of weakness or retreat, but signs of a newly discovered strength to own the truth and feel its pain, which is always the way of advance in life.

Does mourning ever end? In a final sense, where memories of loss never rise or never hurt, probably not. In the sense of no longer managing the whole of life, of stopping progress or derailing recovery, certainly the time of mourning can and does pass. Completing the grieving process can be understood as reaching a place internally where the trauma no longer rules or constrains our sense of identity and self-worth. It means accomplishing acceptance that abuse has happened to us, and wounded us, but it is not who we are. In mourning we let go of things that have hold on us. At some point along the road a survivor comes to know that with head and heart and body.

The Spirituality of Oz

Mourning is a profoundly spiritual matter. Grief exists because we become aware of our mortality and for a brief time we face the ultimate loss of our own self. The losses of the past are gone. They cannot be called back. They belong to death. Grieving, though, is what the living do. Only those who live can cry.

No one who is human can escape being spiritual any more than they can avoid being mortal. However, after my reflections in the last chapter, there may be some among you who cringe to see me again approach the subject of religion and spirituality. You may feel that I, like Nietzsche, consider that the concept of 'God' was invented to oppose life. Nietzsche, in his *Ecce Homo*, finds in the idea of God "everything detrimental, poisonous, and slanderous, and all deadly hostility to life." Such is not my position at all.

Personal spirituality and corporate religious belief and practice are matters of great interest to me. I am convinced that help really is where one finds it. I can scarcely deny the reality of the many people who have benefited immensely from institutional religion, or from their own deep spirituality. I merely maintain that loyalty can blind us to uncomfortable truths about the matters we hold dearest to heart. I make no metaphysical claims here about the reality or nature of God—whether as understood by Christians or anyone else.

My concern is with the *metaphors* by which the dominant religion of our culture has made itself felt and the metaphors we each use to relate ourselves to whatever reality we glimpse standing somewhere beside or beyond our mundane daily existence. At least for some of us, many metaphors must be exchanged for others if we are to find spiritual or religious sources of solace and strength for recovery. Thank goodness metaphors abound.

Generally, what constitutes a great strength has in it seeds of profound weakness. Religion has had the role of preserving a collective conscience for people living together in a society. Religion conserves the wisdom of the past, offering moral guidance, a vision of transcendent reality and future hope, and constantly working to leaven the disruptive forces that seek to destabilize a culture. In these respects, it is difficult to argue with Erich Fromm's wry observation, in *The Dogma of Christ,* that God always seems to be on the side of those who have the power. In this day of Liberation Theologies in the Third World, such an assertion might be challenged. Nevertheless, Fromm's contention that this alliance permits society and religion to utilize each other for social stability has substantial truth.

In this transaction those without power stand to lose the most—and do so most often. In experiencing the wounding of abuse, we may find God enlisted by the abuser to validate the abuse. While I would never contend that any religion worthy of the name condones such an alliance, I do maintain that religion's role in siding with the strong makes the lie plausible to victims. Moreover, I think every religion needs to attend closely to its metaphors to see which ones promote unholy alliances between Power and the misuse of power.

Another obstacle associated with religion, Fromm commented in a dialogue with interviewer Richard Evans, is idolatry. The evil of idolatry is not just that it denigrates God; it demeans us as well. As Fromm saw, in idolatry we transfer our own human powers—qualities such as loving and acting justly—to an idol, effectively diminishing ourselves while simultaneously separating ourselves from God. Fromm also saw what this means: to access our own powers we have to submit to the idol we gave them to!

This is a serious matter and requires us to fully understand it. While virtually everyone knows of idolatry as the substituting of a false god for the true God, not everyone comprehends that even the true God becomes an idol when improperly related to by one who gives up the self in a fruitless effort to possess the divine Other. Jesus' words, "For whoever would save his life will lose it; and whoever loses his life for my sake and the gospel's will save it" (Mark 8:35, RSV), must not be taken as a call to a suicide of self-resourcefulness, competency, and initiative. Idolatry is known precisely by its quality of robbing the full humanity of the worshipper.

If religion is problematic for most of modern humanity, it may be especially so for those of us who found no divine rescue in the midst of our affliction. Of course, others among us may find in faith an anchor against the swirling tides of trauma. If help is where we find it, some find churches, synagogues, mosques, and temples places of shelter, while others find them stumbling blocks. Matters of the spirit are rarely straightforward, and a wounded spirit has needs that many religious institutions find difficult to bind. Some survivors discover that a faith community offers support; others find it offers a cold shoulder to a bleeding heart. And some survivors shudder when they see the signs of faith because such signs were used by their abusers to justify what they did.

Survivors are a community like any other, with some who find solace in religion and others who do not. And some of us find a creative path of our own.

To survive abuse hardly requires abandoning faith. Not all of us become atheists despite our pain, bewilderment, and sense of being abandoned by God. Yet we are likely to be changed by our experience so that our religiosity—or 'spirituality' if we prefer—becomes different from those around us. For those survivors who affirm the Christian faith, some of its elements may sound hollow, or remain elusive, or be given up entirely. To hold on to traditional religion may require of survivors paying a price in belief, practice, or feeling that others are never required to make. Yet other elements of faith, other aspects of belief may surface to compensate for what is lost. Spirituality can prove remarkably resilient.

In truth, regardless of what we experience with religion, we who have passed through the fire of abuse remain spiritual beings no less than others. In fact, many of us discover in our recovery a profound new development of spiritual meaning for our lives. This may follow along lines established by dominant religious traditions or lead us into more esoteric channels. Or it may mean following one's own highly personal muse. Again—help is where one finds it.

Many of us find the renewal of our spirituality outside institutional lines even if, for other reasons, we choose to stay in established religious groups. Perhaps the most common adjunct—or replacement—to traditional, corporate religious experience is the rediscovery of an intensely personal relationship to Nature. Many survivors find in the natural world, that world apart from human interference, a refuge and temple of healing more nurturing than a Church, and more satisfying than what many other people find. Nature is at worst indifferent, and at best benign, where other human beings may be calculatedly evil. In connecting to Nature (which many people image as feminine and thereby balance the patriarchal character of established religions), a person connects with the self, for we are the same stuff as found throughout the universe.

Many of us, young and old, draw special comfort and form particularly significant spiritual connections with certain animals. I have found that horses hold a special appeal to many trauma survivors. Large and powerful, sure of themselves yet self-restrained, independent but congenial, horses may be mirrors of the self we long to be. In attaching to such an animal we may be building an attachment to our own self-image. We have seen the importance of Toto to Dorothy (chapter 9). Who can imagine Dorothy's story without her smallest companion?

How Long?

Earlier we contemplated impatience as a principal obstacle to recovery. Yet the question remains, *how long does recovery take?* The accurate answer may seem so pat as to appear almost trivial, but I know of none better. *Recovery takes as long as it takes.* The simple truth is that there is nothing simple about the process. Everyone's road is different in character and in length.

The one most certain reality is that no one can know how long the road is until it is walked. In a way, it might be comforting to realize that—like a woman giving birth—every labor is unique. In the end, it truly matters little how long recovery takes because the goal is attained and that is all that matters.

Dorothy might faint dead away if she learns in Munchkin Land what lies before her. Fortunately, like the rest of us, the future is shrouded in both promise and challenge for Dorothy. No less than ourselves, she must choose to attend most either to the fear of the challenges ahead—and so stand trembling where she is—or focus on the promises—and thus begin to walk the yellow brick road. And if along the way she finds gaps in the highway, why I imagine she takes time to mix dust with water and build her own bricks.

The Future is Rainbow Bright

"I set my bow in the cloud . . ." (Genesis 9:13; RSV).

In the sacred story tradition shared by the Western religions, a great flood nearly obliterates humanity. But a family survives to repopulate the earth. As a sign from God that never again shall the world be so inundated, rainbows come into existence. At least since then, rainbows have been symbols of promise. They are also markers, separating the passing storm from the bright sunshine now returning. Their cheerful colors are bent like a frown, but who doesn't smile at them? And everyone knows that at their end rests a pot of gold.

Dorothy in Kansas sings wistfully of a land beyond the rainbow. Oz is that land. For survivors of abuse trauma, that land over the rainbow is recovery. It is a place of brilliant technicolor and enchantments both intoxicating and frightening. Somewhere, over the rainbow, Oz waits for those who will come.

Rainbows are born out of a stormy past, light up the present, but beckon our eyes to search the future. Recovery is a process of integrating the past into the present so that the future can grow ever brighter. For victims, the past holds exclusive dominion because the present is so marred by it and the future seems illusory. Yet even victims dream. For survivors, those of us who have renounced our victim status, the past's tyranny is being broken in the present and the future is passing from dream to reality.

None of this, however, is obvious to everyone. There are some who believe survivors focus too much on the past. They worry that this keeps us from living in the present. Others think survivors have trouble staying in the present because we may focus so much energy on the future. After all, the future is where salvation might be; it certainly wasn't in the past, and it seems doubtful in the present.

We have spoken about the hold of the past already. Let's take a minute to regard the allure of the future. Can we focus too much on the future? I believe that is only possible when we fail to preserve a sense of continuity in the self, which comes from a past, occupies the present, and can only intend the future. As long as we remember that the future only exists as a way to inform and steer the present, and not as an independent reality, then we are not likely to go astray. The often repeated urging to "Stay in the present!" does not mean forswearing past and future. Instead, it signifies subordinating the past to the present and keeping in view that the future is only a guiding vision. The real work is always done in the present, for that is where we bodily dwell.

Being conscious of time and mortality often complicates our lives. Erich Fromm, in his dialogue with Evans, remarks that to be born means to encounter the question posed by being alive. Similarly, Viktor Frankl in his *Man's Search for Meaning* advises us that if we are to find meaning we would do better to cease making demands of life and instead ask what life requires of us. I imagine everyone has her or his own way of hearing that question. I know that for myself the question seems to change with time and circumstance.

But at least with regard to how we live in time it seems to me that the question is this: How shall we find a place for our past, trauma and all, so that we are still growing in the present and free to make a future not determined by that past? For me, life requires finding ways to integrate and reintegrate all my experiences so that I can be fully present now and able to walk toward the future without chains holding me back. I want to be able to own my past experience, and carry it with me, without being weighed down by it or stuck with it in the past.

Let us end by a word about hope. The Christian religion puts hope together with faith and love as the three enduring realities (1 Corinthians 13:13). Certainly it merits such status for without hope there can be neither faith nor love. Hope has elements of both confidence and desire. Erik Erikson offers his own words: "Hope is the enduring belief in the attainability of fervent wishes . . . ." For the survivor of trauma there is no more fervent wish than recovery. With great confidence I say to one and all: this is a *realizable* hope. Come, let us walk the road together.

Space for Personal Notes

www.ingramcontent.com/pod-product-compliance
Lightning Source LLC
Chambersburg PA
CBHW030934090426
42737CB00007B/430